FROM THE DECLARATION
OF INDEPENDENCE
TO THE CONSTITUTION

The American Heritage Series
OSKAR PIEST, FOUNDER
. . . .

The American Heritage Series

FROM THE DECLARATION OF INDEPENDENCE TO THE CONSTITUTION

The Roots of American Constitutionalism

Edited, with an introduction, by

CARL J. FRIEDRICH

Eaton Professor of the Science of Government, Harvard University

and

ROBERT G. McCLOSKEY

Professor of Government, Harvard University

· ·

The American Heritage Series

published by

 THE **BOBBS-MERRILL** COMPANY, INC.
A SUBSIDIARY OF HOWARD W. SAMS & CO., INC.
Publishers • INDIANAPOLIS • NEW YORK

CONTENTS
. . . .

THE BASIC DOCUMENTS

I. THE FOUNDATION OF THE UNION

II. THE CONSTITUTION IN THE MAKING

III. THE CONSTITUTION

CONTENTS

THE ROOTS OF AMERICAN CONSTITUTIONALISM

I. THE BACKGROUND OF POLITICAL THOUGHT

It is a common misunderstanding, especially on the part of practical men, to think that great historical events, such as the Declaration of Independence and the efforts at constitution-making which followed it, spring from social life and man's initiative like Athene from the forehead of Zeus. In point of fact, events of this type have a long seed-time during which the ideas crystallize which eventually inform the actions taken. This observation does not oblige one to treat ideas as the only or even the major forces in history. Political and economic, cultural and religious factors all play their vital part alongside the individual human being who is cast in the role of leader. But none of these other factors can come into play, except by being channeled through human thought, and this thought is molded by the ideas prevalent among those who are trying to figure out solutions to the concrete and practical problems confronting them.

The seeds which germinated before the American Revolution and burst forth into the great documents here under consideration were gathered over a long period of time. Indeed, some of the crucial ones, such as that "men are created equal," trace to the beginnings of Christianity and to the great thinkers of classical antiquity. That a good government should be a "government of laws and not of men" is a rhetorical exaggeration of the Aristotelian (as well as late Platonic) notion that a government should be operating according to law, and was so operating whenever it was ethically sound. But it would be manifestly impossible to trace the basic ideas of Western political thought embedded in the American Declaration of Independence and the Constitution throughout the many centuries of their unfolding. Nor is it necessary to do so, because the more particular form which they were to take in these documents is more profitably studied in the thinkers of the seventeenth and eighteenth centuries. For it is in these writers, such as Hooker, Harrington and Locke, Pufendorf and Montesquieu, that these ideas found the kind of expression that made sense to the American Founding Fathers. It was these writers whom they read and quoted, and it was their experience—more especially English traditional constitutionalism—which they knew about and believed themselves to be a part of.

It has been said, and not without justice, that the American Revolution, in spite of its lively relation to the French Revolution, is in many respects an echo of the English Revolution of the seventeenth century. Certainly many of the English revolutionaries, including the great Cromwell himself, had considered going to America in order to found there the kind of Godly Commonwealth which they eventually tried to bring into existence in England. More importantly perhaps, the dominant problem of the English Revolution, namely how to bring into being a rationally conceived and consciously framed and adopted constitution, was an idea which the three revolutions shared, at least at the outset. Interestingly enough, only the American Revolution succeeded in carrying through to success a task which so radically clashed with all notions of a traditional order of society. This result was not due to any inherent difference in the ideas they espoused, but in the conditions under which their application was attempted. As Louis Hartz has well said, "In America one not only found a society sufficiently fluid to give a touch of meaning to the individualistic norm of Locke, but one also found letter-perfect replicas of the very images he used. There was a frontier that was a veritable state of nature. There were agreements, such as the Mayflower Compact, that were veritable social contracts." [1]

[1] Louis Hartz, "American Political Thought and the American Revolution," *American Political Science Review*, XLVI, 338.

1. The General Idea of Constitutionalism

The idea of constitutionalism in the distinct Western sense was slowly distilled in the course of English revolutionary developments. Its antecedents reach back to the medieval doctrine of the supremacy of law. But only when this "law" was understood as something man-made and consciously conceived and explicitly formulated to deal with specific issues did it posit the problem of constitutionalism in its characteristic modern form. The traditional English notions are expressed in terms of a legislative power exercised by the "King in Parliament." In this form, they find their place in the political thought of Sir John Fortescue, Sir Thomas Smith and Sir Edward Coke.[2] All three of them are disinclined to differentiate the legislative function very precisely from the judicial function, and this has given rise to acrimonious debate among scholars. Some have held that the idea of "parliamentary sovereignty" was clearly embraced by Sir Thomas Smith; [3] others have denied that there is any clear differentiation between the judicial and the legislative at all.[4] Neither of these views is right. In point of fact, Smith expounded what Harrington came to call "modern prudence"—a scheme of constitutional government in which the legislative power, considered supremely important, is entrusted to a corporate entity consisting of the "estate" of the King, and the two further "estates" of the lords and commons, all of which Smith believes to be "present" in the great court of parliament which represents all England collectively. The problem of supremacy—or, as it

[2] Cf. Sir John Fortescue, *Governance of England* (1471?) and *De Laudibus Legum Angliae* (1468-70, publ. 1537); Sir Thomas Smith, *De Republica Anglorum* (1565, publ. 1583); Sir Edward Coke, *Institutes* (1628-44), esp. Vol. IV.

[3] Cf. F. W. Maitland, *Constitutional History of England* (1908), pp. 254ff. Sir James Bryce, *Studies in History and Jurisprudence* (1901), I, pp. 553f.

[4] Cf. Charles H. McIlwain, *The High Court of Parliament and its Supremacy* (1910), pp. 124ff., and L. Alston, "Introduction" to his edition of *De Republica Anglorum* (1906), pp. xxviiff.

was spoken of on the Continent, that of sovereignty—had not clearly been seen, nor was it acknowledged until after Coke's time, that is to say, after the settlement of North America had commenced. When the Declaration of Independence came to speak of King George III as a tyrant and of his government as an "absolute despotism," based on usurpations, it really spoke in terms of this ancient tradition, as Professor McIlwain has so persuasively shown in his *The American Revolution*.[5] Yet, the American revolutionaries could never have spoken as they did, had they been attached only to this tradition, because that tradition did not recognize any right of revolution, except in terms of the vague medieval sanction against a tyranny that had first to be ecclesiastically recognized and condemned. It was a long road that led from the traditional and essentially legalistic constitutionalism to the rational constitutionalism of John Locke. This road lay through a veritable valley of sweat, blood and tears. But we need not traverse this valley in this introduction, because the great events of the English Revolution were already events of the distant past when the Declaration of Independence was drafted and proclaimed. Those who did draft and proclaim it read Locke rather than Hooker, and Montesquieu rather than Sir Thomas Smith. They were "enlightened" and "rational" in the eighteenth-century way. But unless one appreciates what lay beyond in the seventeenth century and even earlier, he is apt to miss the deeper roots of American revolutionary thought.

John Locke's conception of constitutionalism rests firmly upon the basis of a rational law of nature. This rational law of nature is a law of self-preservation, but the desire for self-preservation is not an anxiety-ridden neurosis in the manner of Hobbes, but is tempered by man's desire for social intercourse and happiness. In this connection, Locke stresses the preservation of property as a very essential feature both of

[5] Cf. Charles H. McIlwain, *The American Revolution: A Constitutional Interpretation* (1904). His view was contested, but not convincingly, as far as the present argument is concerned, by Robert L. Schuyler, *Parliament and the British Empire* (1929).

self-preservation and happiness. When Jefferson came to pen the famous triad of "life, liberty and the pursuit of happiness" (in lieu of life, liberty and property, as well as happiness, as the Virginia Bill of Rights [June 12, 1776] had it), he did not make as much of a change from Locke as is sometimes supposed. In Locke the lines between happiness and property are fluid, partly because property does not in his *Second Treatise* have the narrow modern meaning of material possessions or even of a "bundle of relations," [6] but means instead all that rightfully belongs to a man, and hence constitutes the ineluctable source of such happiness as he may achieve. Because of this concern with self-preservation, man readily enters into society so as to make secure these ends in peaceful association with others who are similarly motivated.

Men being, as has been said, by nature all free, equal, and independent, no one can be put out of his estate and subjected to the political power of another without his own consent, which is done by agreeing with other men, to join and unite into a community for their comfortable, safe, and peaceable living, one amongst another, in a secure enjoyment of their properties, and a greater security against any that are not of it. . . . And thus every man, by consenting with others to make one body politic under one government, puts himself under an obligation to every one of that society to submit to the determination of the majority, and to be concluded by it . . .[7]

This constituent act by which a political society comes into existence and a civil government is formed is crucial for the Lockean scheme of things. It stems from the Puritan faith in a fundamental covenant, such as the Pilgrim Fathers executed on the Mayflower. The terms of this compact are strictly in line with the thinking that culminated in Locke, a kind of thinking which dominated the revolutionary leaders in Britain until Cromwell despaired of his efforts at bringing

[6] Walton Hamilton, "Property," in *Encyclopedia of the Social Sciences.*
[7] Locke, *The Second Treatise of Government,* edited by Thomas P. Peardon, ("The Library of Liberal Arts," No. 31, [New York: The Liberal Arts Press, Inc.]), Section 95, pp. 54-55.

into existence a constitution built around a formally divided legislative. The "Agreement of the People" (1647) has frequently been hailed as perhaps the first modern "constitution." It was a growing conviction among Puritans and other Englishmen that a civil government could be instituted by fiat of the constituent will of the people, based upon rational principles of government. If such rational principles could be discovered to be embodied in a traditional system, so much the better for all concerned. Locke's triumphant demonstration that this was the case in England had much to do with the vogue of his treatise.

But Locke had laid the foundation for the American enterprise. We read in the Declaration of Independence that "in the course of human events, it becomes necessary for one people to dissolve the political bands which have connected them with another," and furthermore that it may also become necessary "to assume among the Powers of the earth, the separate and equal station to which the Laws of Nature and Nature's God entitle them." Such phrases were indeed an echo of Locke's statement of the right of revolution. "There are," he wrote, "no examples so frequent in history as those of men withdrawing themselves and their obedience from the jurisdiction they were born under . . . and setting up new governments in other places . . .," [8] and again he asserted that no man or society of men has "a power to deliver up their preservation, or consequently the means of it, to the absolute will and arbitrary dominion of another," [9] and therefore whenever anyone shall go about to bring them into "such a slavish condition" they always "have a right to preserve what they have not a power to part with." [10] Therefore they may "rid themselves of those who invade this fundamental, sacred and unalterable law of self-preservation." [11]

This self-preservation was closely bound up with the right of private property. Property had a very broad meaning, as we just showed, but it also had the very specific and narrow

[8] *Ibid.*, Sec. 115, p. 66.   [9] *Ibid.*, Sec. 149, p. 85.
[10] *Loc. cit.*   [11] *Loc. cit.*

meaning which is associated with it today. To take property without a man's consent was one of the most heinous acts of arbitrary government; whether this act was agreed to by a parliament or not was of little consequence, when that parliament did not represent those whose property was being taken. Locke is insistent upon this point, even though he stresses at the same time the binding obligation springing from the decision of the majority once a man has come to acquiesce in his role as a member of the community.

At this point, Harrington's thought supplemented Locke's in providing an armory for the revolutionaries. For whereas Locke in spite of his general recognition of the right of revolution had stayed essentially within the framework of traditional English constitutionalism, Harrington constructed his *Commonwealth of Oceana* (1656) from rational principles, as he perceived them, without any concern for the traditional pattern. We find in Harrington an analysis of the problem of government that leads him to the well-known statement that a commonwealth consists of "the senate proposing, the people resolving, and the magistracy executing." He interprets this in the classical tradition as a "mixed form of government," partaking of aristocracy, democracy and monarchy, and therefore "complete." [12] A commonwealth is, for Harrington, always a "government of laws, and not of men." He never wearies of repeating this basic insight, which assigns to the wise and intellectually superior the role of discussing the problems, to the people as the compound of all the divergent interests the role of making the basic decisions, and to the magistrates the task of enforcing and executing these decisions. It is evident that once representation of the people in a popular assembly is added, the American scheme of a government based upon the separation of powers is delineated. This government comes into existence by the people's constituent act when they organize the government in accordance with these principles.

[12] James Harrington, *The Commonwealth of Oceana* (ed. Toland, 1700), pp. 48ff.

2. The Separation of Powers

Such then was the nature of the concept of constitutionalism which America had evolved from the speculations and practices of the past. A second cornerstone of the edifice of political ideas which America had constructed was the idea of separation of powers, and it therefore becomes important to sketch the way in which this doctrine developed prior to its reception by the writers of America's fundamental law.

The idea of the separation of powers emerges from the much older notion of a mixed form of government which goes back to Plato and Aristotle and was elaborated by Polybius. It is fascinating to watch this ancient idea being transformed into the related but different modern concept. The role of the English parliament is vital in this connection, as is the emergence of the emphasis upon legislation already noted. For Locke, the real concern is not that of separating the powers or functions (which had actually been more clearly divided by Sir Thomas Smith), but of dividing the legislative power, because it is so very important. What is of primary importance is to prevent the legislative power from being abused, and that can only be done by making king, lords and commons share in its exercise. The other two powers or functions which Locke identifies, namely, the "executive" and the "federative," are not so important; hence he is quite content to entrust them to the monarch, who also possesses a residual power of the "prerogative." This rather primitive scheme of a separation of powers was radically revised and rationalized by Montesquieu. Montesquieu has often been taken to task for not perceiving the emergent pattern of British parliamentary government. Such critics overlook that this scheme of things was actually looked upon by many of the contemporaries as a kind of corruption,[1] and certainly was not very fully developed, let alone stabilized and legitimized when Mon-

[1] E.g., Henry St. John, Viscount Bolingbroke, *A Dissertation Upon Parties* (1733-4).

tesquieu went to England to observe the workings of British government. In any case, Montesquieu cherished a preconceived notion in favor of an independent judiciary, such as he himself knew in France and which was still operative there, though in a very limited way. Locke had not emphasized the judicial power. To him, it was rather important to stress the legislative authority of parliament, and so he assigned to the crown most of the judicial power under the heading: "execution of the laws." [2] Montesquieu was most determined to vindicate the separate status and basic importance of this power of which he wrote the famous description that it is *"dans une façon nul,"* that is to say, in a certain sense "nothing." [3] Now, as a matter of fact, there had taken place in England's constitutional evolution a step which fitted right into Montesquieu's notions and that was the Act of Settlement by which the judiciary was made independent through the well-known injunction that judges hold their office *quamdiu se bene gesserint,* ("as long as they conduct themselves well"). So Montesquieu would seem to have been justified in modifying the Lockean scheme by a clear recognition of this power as separate and distinct.

Now while the executive power becomes the judicial power, the federative power which in Locke's system had been the power of war and peace, that is to say, over foreign policy, is by Montesquieu expanded to become the executive power. This Montesquieu accomplished by associating the problem of internal with that of external security and thus merging the idea of police methods for maintaining internal peace and order with the idea of devising means for insuring safety from external aggression. This new executive power corresponded of course much more nearly with modern conceptions than Locke's, and indeed it was derived from and informed by continental European politics and government in the days of benevolent despotism and mercantilism.

[2] Cf. Locke, *op. cit.,* Sec. 143, 147, 149-156.

[3] Charles de Secondat, Baron de Montesquieu, *Spirit of the Laws,* transl. by Thomas Nugent, XI, Ch. VI.

This distinction of the several functions is in fact rationally based upon the differentiation of the types of decisions which man is called upon to make, namely, to formulate general rules, to adopt specific and particular actions or measures, and to adjudicate between conflicting interpretations of general rules in their application to particular situations.[4] It deeply impressed the American constitution-makers, who made it an underlying premise of the American constitutional pattern and quoted it extensively in the debates as well as in justificatory writings, such as *The Federalist* afterwards. This has obscured the fact that Montesquieu almost by a sleight of hand transformed Locke's reasoned argument about the importance of dividing the legislative power (because of its inherent importance!) into the contention that liberty required the separation of these several functions from each other and the vesting of them in separate and distinct persons or bodies of persons. Thus an argument against the concentration of the legislative power in one hand became an argument against the concentrating of the three powers in one hand, but with the corollary presumption that the legislative power might just as well be in the hands of one person or group of persons. The merger of this notion with the older notion of legislative supremacy has led to a construction which has recurrently threatened the United States with the patent evils of "Congressional government." [5]

When eventually John Adams came to elaborate the ideas of Montesquieu in terms of a complex pattern of separated and mutually checked and balanced powers, it became clear that the fear of government had become so great that the separation of powers was now very nearly the concept of a state of nature.[6] Ardent believer in orderly government that

---

[4] For further details see Friedrich, *Constitutional Government and Democracy* (1951), Ch. X.

[5] Cf. Thomas Woodrow Wilson, *Congressional Government* (1885).

[6] Cf. John Adams, *A Defence of the Constitutions of Government of the United States of America* (1786-8). Cf. also Zoltán Harazti, *John Adams and the Prophets of Progress* (1952), esp. Ch. VIII.

he was, his various governmental powers appear to be so completely occupied with checking and balancing each other that
little power is left for the primary task of governing. The same
passionate faith in the constructive powers of society as against
the purely repressive function of government is set forth by
Thomas Paine. "Society in every state is a blessing," he proclaimed in *Common Sense* (1775), "but government, even in its
best state, is but a necessary evil, in its worst state an intoler-
able one . . ." [7] The ringing phrases of the pamphlet culminate in a very DECLARATION FOR INDEPENDENCE which
stems from a withering attack upon the British constitution. The British constitution is described as a senseless
compound of "remains of monarchical tyranny," "remains of
aristocratical tyranny," and "republican materials." [8] It is "so
"exceedingly complex" that no one knows what he is at.
"To say that the Constitution of England is a *union* of three
powers, reciprocally *checking* each other, is farcical; either the
words have no meaning, or they are flat contradictions." [9]

He explores this farce, he surveys the recent conflict with
Britain, and he cries out: "Everything that is right or reasonable pleads for separation. The blood of the slain, the weep-
ing voice of nature cries, *'Tis time to part.*" [10] He reinforced
this thought later in his *Rights of Man* (1791—first published
in French) . "The continual use of the word *Constitution* in
the English Parliament shows there is none . . . if there were a
constitution, it certainly could be referred to; and the debate
on any constitutional point would terminate by producing the
constitution." [11] Here we have the conceit of many writers and
thinkers of the time, the result of their lack of semantic so-
phistication: if you write a constitution, its meaning will be
self-evident. Paine speaks for a wide-spread movement in Eng-

[7] *Thomas Paine, Common Sense and Other Political Writings,* edited
by Nelson F. Adkins, ("The American Heritage Series," No. 5, [New
York: The Liberal Arts Press, Inc.]), p. 4.
[8] *Ibid.,* p. 7.   [9] *Ibid.*   [10] *Ibid.,* p. 23.
[11] *Rights of Man,* Part I, "Miscellaneous Chapter," (cf. *Thomas Paine,*
edited by Harry Hayden Clark [New York: American Book Company]),
p. 151.

land and on the Continent. Americans, in acting upon it, were not doing something out of line with prevailing European thought, but distinctly intended to be an expression of it.

The argument which Paine is combating is of course that of Burke. Burke had exalted the British constitution, based upon the prescription of long usage; Burke had denounced the proclamation of abstract rights in the name of a presumption in favor of long established privilege.[12] Said Paine:

Every age and generation must be free to act for itself, *in all cases,* as the ages and generations which preceded it. The vanity and presumption of governing beyond the grave is the most ridiculous and insolent of tyrannies.[13]

Government is man-created, and man will do away with it when it fails to do what it was set up to do. In keeping with Locke's already considered opinion, Paine claimed that "the instant formal government is abolished, society begins to act. A general association takes place, and common interest produces common security." [14] Formal government, he thought, made but a small part of civilized life and "the more perfect a civilization is, the less occasion has it for government, because the more does it regulate its own affairs, and govern itself . . ." [15] In these radical pronouncements, a clearly anarchic strain appears; somehow a free association is pictured as capable of effective action; yet at another point he himself acknowledges "that government is nothing more than a national association acting on the principles of society." [16]

3. The Natural Rights of Man

Now among these principles of society, the most important in the eyes of the American revolutionaries, no less than in those of Thomas Paine, were the natural rights of man, and the concept of rights is the third premise of American political thought which we must consider. The Declaration of Inde-

[12] Edmund Burke, *Reflections upon the Revolution in France* (1790).
[13] *Thomas Paine, Common Sense and Other Political Writings,* (Adkins), pp. 76-77.
[14] *Ibid.,* p. 117.   [15] *Ibid.*   [16] *Ibid.,* p. 120.

pendence is explicit on the subject, and the Constitution was not adopted until the addition of a Bill of Rights was pledged. We have already remarked that this idea goes back to the English Revolution of the seventeenth century. It is interwoven with the idea of a natural law which comes down from classical antiquity, as we have seen. The great age of natural law had been the preceding century and a half, however. From Grotius to Hume, natural law had offered itself not only as a principle for justifying revolution, as in Locke, but as a principle for justifying absolute authority and monarchical government. Indeed, by the time the Declaration was composed, natural law had become a commonplace of general argumentation and its philosophical foundation had been undermined by Hume. From it, Thomas Hobbes had deduced a long list of rules of prudence, and the absolutists of a later day had sought to argue from it for some rational restraint to be observed by benevolent rulers.

But the key idea was that of the sacred sphere of human right which no government invades but at its peril. The toleration which John Locke preached was but a concluding sermon in which a century's protracted arguments over religious freedom were summed up, just as his spirited defense of the right of private property summarized the notions concerning economic freedom that had developed in the struggle against royal absolutism. It was only natural that once the right of freedom in the sphere of religion and property should have crystallized, others should make their appearance. These rights which were set forth in most of the state constitutions framed after the Declaration of Independence were always treated as inherent, that is to say, as basically related to man's very being and dignity. Certain procedural safeguards had already figured prominently in the days of Sir Edward Coke, had been the center of the Petition of Rights (1628) and continued to be looked upon as a "birthright" of all Englishmen. Thus the right of an accused to be brought before a judge and to hear what is the accusation levelled against him, to be confronted with witnesses, to have a speedy trial by an impartial jury, and to be free from compulsion to give evidence against himself—in short, that a man may not be "deprived of his Liberty except by the Law of the Land, or the Judgment of his Peers," as the ancient formula went—all these rights were now linked with the religious and property rights into one comprehensive package. To it were added freedom from searches and seizures, and even the freedom of the press and of peaceable assembly, among others.

The recognition of these basic rights is intimately associated, of course, with the rise of constitutionalism and its theory. Only when the idea of a limited government had firmly taken root, could the concept of such rights be fully implemented. The very complaints which the Declaration voiced as demonstrating the tyrannical character of the rule of George III are formulated as violations of these rights. The most comprehensive philosophy of these rights in terms of natural law was formulated by the philosopher Christian Wolff, who in his *Institutions of the Law of Nature and Nations* (1750) noted equality and a right not only of security and self-defense, but also of punishing a wrong-doer. His thought traces clearly back to Locke. The trenchant criticism levelled by Hume at the concept of natural law and rights seems little to have affected the writers of the Constitution. In John Adams' view, Hume was a "wise fool, a learned idiot, a profound, deep-thinking coxcomb," [1] but Hamilton thought him "solid and ingenuous (sic)." [2]

[1] Haraszti, *op. cit.*, p. 214.

[2] Cf. *The Federalist*, No. 85, where Hamilton quotes the following passage: "To balance a large state or society, whether monarchical or republican, on general laws is a work of so great difficulty that no human genius, however comprehensive, is able by the mere dint of reason and reflection to effect it. The judgments of many must unite in this work; experience must guide their labor; time must bring it to perfection; and the feeling of inconveniences must correct the mistakes which they inevitably fall into in their first trials and experiments." (From "Of the Rise and Progress of the Arts and Sciences," reprinted in *David Hume's Political Essays* ["The Library of Liberal Arts," No. 34, New York: The Liberal Arts Press, Inc.]), pp. 111ff.

Georg Jellinek has argued persuasively that the preceding natural law doctrines and the ideas of the enlightenment were insufficient for explaining the idea that these rights should be solemnly *declared*. Stressing the Lockean antecedents is not enough. In such a work as James Otis' *The Rights of the Colonies Asserted and Proved* (1764), these rights are transformed, so Jellinek insists, into *"subjective* rights." [3] These rights are not conferred by the state, but are possessed by the individual against the state. And since England sought to invade them, the idea now appears that these rights should be solemnly proclaimed. It was so done at Boston in 1772, and again at Philadelphia in 1774. It is to be doubted, however, whether the distinction between objective and subjective rights is really important. The Petition of Rights in 1628 had stated the four rights which it vindicated as rights of all free Englishmen and had solemnly proclaimed them. But the Declaration in America broadened them from the prescriptive rights of Englishmen into human rights of universal application.

4. Federalism

The Articles of Confederation and the Constitution are both built upon the idea of federalism, and it is worth inquiring whether there are significant antecedents for this important doctrine. It is often alleged that federalism constitutes a wholly novel attack upon problems of government, especially as propounded in *The Federalist*. No one would have been more surprised than Madison to hear any such claim made. For he made an extensive review of past federal experience and *The Federalist* shows very clear signs of the Constitution having been written in the light of these experiences and their theoretical formulations.

The theory of federalism is a difficult subject. Gierke has linked it with the Germanic corporate theories of free and

[3] Georg Jellinek, *Die Erklärung der Menschen- und Bürgerrechte* (4th ed.; 1927), Ch. IX, esp. pp. 66ff.

cooperative associations.[1] There can be little doubt that some medieval writers, notably the conciliarists, adumbrated a kind of federal theory. The notion of a federal structure of political society was made by Johannes Althusius [2] the center of his doctrine of state and sovereignty. He saw the commonwealth as an organic structure, rising from a free association of families into guilds, a free association of guilds into towns, of towns into provinces, and of provinces into a commonwealth. The right of the community to build its own governmental structure rested upon this free association of interrelated groups. In contrast to most of the writers of the seventeenth and eighteenth centuries, who could only conceive of unitary states and of leagues of such states, Althusius provided for a genuine theory by which to comprehend such entities as the United Netherlands and Switzerland. As is well known, the makers of the American constitution were much interested in both.

But there is no hint that any of them had ever heard of Althusius, in spite of the fact that he was the most comprehensive political theorist ever produced by orthodox Calvinism. His work had been buried by generations of neglect. Instead, they had before them the theory of the importance of intermediary powers, which Montesquieu had developed. Althusius had held that without them a monarchy was apt to turn into a despotism, which suited the colonial frame of mind well, but did not really amount to a full-blown theory of federalism. Indeed, had such a theory existed at the time, it might have served, as it does nowadays, to provide the underpinning for a federal association with the mother country. But the idea of popular sovereignty which we have examined, when combined with the right of revolution and basic rights, spelled independence rather than federal bonds.

The modern theory of federalism arose from the compro-

---

[1] Otto v. Gierke, *Johannes Althusius und die Entwicklung der naturrechtlichen Staatstheorien* (1888 and later), trans. by Freyd under the title, *The Development of Political Theory* (1939), Ch. V.

[2] Cf. C. J. Friedrich, *Politica Methodica Digesta of Johannes Althusius*, esp. the Introduction (1933).

mises which were worked out in the course of the constitutional labors at Philadelphia. These compromises themselves were not the result of theoretical speculations, but of a hardheaded concern with the practical exigencies. What the constitution-makers aimed at was a federal union strong enough to provide an effective government, and yet limited enough to leave ample scope to the several states for a political life of their own. This, of course, had been precisely the aim of those who undertook to build up the Swiss Confederation and later the United Provinces of the Netherlands. Hence their practical experience was valuable; in fact it embedded the kind of earlier constitutional thinking that had interested Althusius, who studied in Switzerland and spent most of his life in the city of Emden, which was closely associated with the Netherlands. Indeed, his theories were so congenial to the Dutch that they made several efforts to secure his services. So a thread runs to the American constitution from these earlier efforts, but it is a thin one.

5. The Problem of Democracy

If federalism emerged from the constitutional work done at Philadelphia, the same cannot be said with equal certainty of democracy. The later development of the United States into the largest and most powerful democracy ever to come into existence has tended to obscure the fact that it was not so at the beginning. Indeed, the makers of the Constitution were sharply divided on the issue. Many of them shared the eighteenth-century prejudice against democracy (see below). Notably Hamilton, but others as well, thought of the people as a rather dubious repository of political power; *The Federalist* is full of such animadversions as the "gusts of popular passion" and the like. But there were others, of course, notably Benjamin Franklin, who wanted a democratic constitution and did their best to secure it.

Democracy had not, until then, been a highly regarded form

of government. The excesses of the French revolutionary ter-
ror, committed in its name, were to give it a black eye for another generation or more in France and elsewhere. The leading men of the American colonies had been raised in the aristocratic tradition of England, and when they spoke of the
"people" in political theory, they meant the better classes
represented in the Commons in England, not by any means
"the common man." And yet, democratic thought and feeling
had worked themselves into the thought and feeling of the
Americans. It was partly a matter of their living the hard but
free and independent life of the frontiersmen and settlers. But
it was also their close community relations in towns and vil-
lages where the word "neighbor" spelled much more common
effort than it does in settled countries. Finally, the dominant
position of the congregational churches in New England con-
tributed their part to the general atmosphere, reinforced as
it was by the many sectarian elements which had sought refuge
in the rather tolerant colonies overseas. The active efforts of
such men as William Penn had added to this natural inclina-
tion an explicit inducement.

The democratic ideas and the ferment associated with them
cannot be traced in such evident lineage as can those derived
from Locke and beyond. Antecedents there are, and plenty of
them, but they are dispersed and often indirect. Luther's stress
upon the wickedness of government, as of all worldly affairs,
derived from St. Augustine, seems somehow mirrored in the
doubts about all government which animated such diverse
thinkers as Paine and Adams; it also seems somehow involved
in the rising democratic sentiment, even though Luther can
scarcely be called a democrat. Paine's universally acclaimed
faith in society, as contrasted with government, may be seen
in this perspective as a secular form of the old notion of an
invisible church, so dear to the heart of the reformers, as a
substitute for the universal church of the Middle Ages.

Perhaps the most explicit statement of democratic theory
had occurred in England in the course of the Revolution. We

have referred to the Agreement of the People [1] before. "That in all laws made or to be made every person may be bound alike, and that no tenure, estate, charter, degree, birth, or place do confer any exemption from the ordinary course of legal proceedings whereunto others are subjected . . ."—this equality before the law was one of the native rights stressed there. But the Levellers [2] carried the idea further. The dominant elements, more especially Cromwell, did not accept such notions. John Milton and other ideologues like Harrington bitterly denounced democratic leanings as destructive of a commonwealth. But quite a few of those who had a penchant in this direction went across to America. In John Lilburne's writings we find much of what was alive in America as democratic principles by the time of the Declaration. In his *The Free-man's Freedom Vindicated* (1646) we find such sharp phrasings as this: "And unnatural, irrational, sinful, wicked, unjust, devilish, and tyrannical, it is for any man whatsoever, spiritual or temporal, clergyman or layman, to appropriate and assume unto himself a power, authority, or jurisdiction, to rule, govern or reign over any sort of men in the world without their free consent, . . ." This was not a generic consent, either, of a people composed of the upper classes, but the mass of the simple folks portrayed in *Pilgrim's Progress*.[3] Time and time again the Levellers raised their voices for all the common people of England against first the elite of the Presbyterian parliamentarians and then the revolutionary elite of Cromwell and his commonwealth-men. The Council of the

[1] An agreement between the Independents and the Levellers in 1649 outlining a common program of principles and action in pursuing the aims of the Revolution. (Cf. *Puritanism and Liberty*, edited by A. S. P. Woodehouse, [Chicago: The University of Chicago Press, 1951]), p. 444.

[2] A party which arose in the army of the Long Parliament about 1647, left of center. More radical and more secular in their political thinking than the Independents, the Levellers advocated a levelling of all ranks. (Cf. Woodehouse, *op. cit.*, esp. the Introduction.)

[3] Bunyan's *Pilgrim's Progress From This World to That Which is to Come*.

Army had been a genuine assembly: here the cry was raised by the common soldier that "the poorest he that is in England hath a life to live, as the greatest he." [4]

These trends appeared likewise, of course, in colonial New England. Thomas Hooker,[5] who had fled from England, is one of those who spoke for democracy. "Many freemen grew very jealous of their liberties," a contemporary says of his influence. He opposed Governor John Winthrop's elitism; Hooker wrote that "in matters of greater importance, which concerns the common good, a general counsel chosen by all, I conceive, under favour, most suitable to rule. . . ." [6] More outspoken still was the position of Roger Williams.[7] Vernon Parrington describes him as the inspired anticipator of much that was to come later.[8] It seems equally true that this democratic radical stands as a living sign of much that was implicit in the Puritan heritage, much that was to unfold in slower minds under the hospitable skies of a free America. Roger Williams was, in short, an original thinker who could make explicit what was present as germ. He was primarily a political philosopher who embraced the basic conceptions of democracy without cavil. ". . . the Soveraigne, originall, and foundation of civill power lies in the people . . . and if so, that a People may erect and establish what forme of government seemes to them most meete for their civill condition. . . ." [9] And in the same vein again:

Every lawful magistrate, whether succeeding or elective, is not only the Minister of God, but the Minister or servant of the people also (what people or nation soever they be all the world over), and that Minister or Magistrate goes beyond his

---

[4] Thomas Rainborough, "Army Debates at Putney 1647." (Cf. Woodehouse, *op. cit.*, p. 53.)

[5] Thomas Hooker, *A Survey of the Summe of Church-Discipline*, Introduction.

[6] Quoted by V. L. Parrington, *Main Currents*, I, 58.

[7] Most important is his *The Bloudy Tenent of Persecution for Cause of Conscience, discussed in a Conference between Truth and Peace* (1644).

[8] Parrington, *op. cit.*, pp. 62-75, see esp. p. 62.

[9] Williams, *op. cit.*, Ch. XCII.

commission who intermeddles with that which cannot be given him in commission from the people . . .[10]

Ideas such as these were expounded by an ever-expanding stream of voices in Colonial America, including the non-Puritan colonies of the South, until by the time Jefferson came to compose the Declaration they had swollen into a mighty chorus. That is why Jefferson could later say that these ideas seemed to be "the common sense of the matter."

If one reviews the over-all course of American thought as embodied in the Declaration of Independence, the Articles of Confederation and the Constitution, one is bound to conclude that the ideas are not new. Whether one considers constitutionalism as such, or the related notions of a separation of powers, rationally based, of human rights derived from natural law, of federalism, and of democracy, they are part and parcel of the great heritage of Christian Europe. As Carl Becker has said, in his remarkable study of *The Declaration of Independence,*

In political theory and in political practice the American Revolution drew its inspiration from the parliamentary struggle of the seventeenth century. The philosophy of the Declaration was not taken from the French. It was not even new; but good old English doctrine newly formulated to meet a present emergency.[11]

This fact of its linkage with the European heritage is not a weakness but a point of decided strength, in the past as well as at the present time and in the future.

6. The Pre-revolutionary Controversy

The course of history that culminated in the Declaration of Independence and the Constitution can be traced back, as we have seen, to its roots in the ancient tradition of the western world; but the immediate stimulus for this upsurge of revo-

10 *The Bloudy Tenent yet more Bloudy* (reprinted in "Narrangansett Club Publications," IV, 187).

11 Carl Becker, *The Declaration of Independence* (1942), p. 79.

lution and creation was provided by a series of events that began about 1763. In that year Great Britain emerged victorious from the long war with France, and her rulers, looking about them, saw that the island kingdom had become an indubitable world empire. And satisfying though it might be for the patriotic Englishman to contemplate the glories of imperial status, it was also evident to him that his country's achievement brought formidable problems in its wake. An empire cannot be merely enjoyed; it must be defended as well; and it seemed only reasonable to ask that the American colonists share not only the laurels of victory but its burdens. The British ministry needed increased revenue to help defray the costs of imperial organization; quite naturally, their thoughts turned to a program for tightening and increasing the taxes on their thriving American colonies.

Nominal taxes on America's external trade had been in force for many years, but colonial merchants had been accustomed to evade or ignore them, and Britain had heretofore made no effective efforts to enforce them strictly. Now the loopholes in this tax procedure were tightened up, and in 1764 the revenue system was supplemented by the Sugar Act, which levied import duties on a number of commodities. These measures were highly distasteful to the colonists, but Parliament's authority to adopt them was beyond serious question, and opposition was fairly moderate in temper. In the next year, however, Parliament passed the Stamp Act, which imposed duties on papers employed in common business transactions. This tax, though hardly a burden in its immediate incidence, contrasted with the preceding measure in one all-important respect: it was directed not at external but at internal trade and thus involved the inevitable implication that parliamentary authority extended to matters which the colonists had been accustomed to regard as their own exclusive concerns. The violent storm of protest that arose from America must have puzzled and astonished the policy-makers in Whitehall and should have given them cause to reconsider with care the nature of the people who inhabited Britain's New World outpost. For almost a century the mother country had pursued toward the colonies a policy that Burke called "salutary neglect," and America, as might have been expected, had developed a national character while England was looking the other way. Now the American mind was emerging to take its place on the stage of world history, and some knowledge of it is important to an understanding of the institutions it fashioned.

The American spirit, as the British ministry might have perceived had it troubled to examine the matter, had become something very dissimilar to the England of George III. It was a complex of diverse strains and influences, many of them drawn from England in the first instance, to be sure, but shaped and tempered for the past 150 years in a quite different crucible. It was a spirit rich in strange virtues and—to the Englishman—even stranger prejudices, ridden by a multiplicity of contradictions which accounted at once for its attributes and its deficiencies. Like John Adams, who became one of the makers of the Revolution and the second President of the United States, America was both vain and unsure of herself. Like Benjamin Franklin, who skilfully represented the American cause abroad and earned the deep respect of Europe's two most powerful capitals, the nascent republic was both homespun and philosophic, both pragmatic and speculative. Like John Dickinson, who helped foment the revolution with his pamphleteering, then opposed the Declaration of Independence, and finally enlisted as a private in the revolutionary army, the American mind was at one and the same time staunchly traditionalistic and profoundly libertarian. And above all, like Thomas Jefferson, who was to write the Declaration and to hold nearly every important public office in the gift of his country, that country was content to live with her inconsistencies rather than to resolve them.

To understand these characteristics—and most particularly the last—is to understand much about the history of the three decades that followed the Stamp Act and not a little about the subsequent development of the nation. Conceptual patterns that are sound enough when applied to other data break down when we seek to impose them on the intellectual history of the United States. The familiar story of thesis and antithesis struggling toward synthesis is doubly false for America, first because the cleavages such a viewpoint postulates so often turn out to be agreements when we examine them closely; and secondly, because the contradictions that do exist are tolerated and allowed to live side by side in the American mind. It is not quite correct to say that the American spirit was indifferent to its diversities; when a contradiction was capable of easy resolution, then America gladly resolved it. But when a synthesis seemed unnecessary or difficult, or both, there was no restless drive to press forward to accomplish it in the name of consistency. Rather, America was prone to let the discrepancies stand, joined together in a marriage of opposites that would have made a more logical people desperately uneasy.

Nowhere are these characteristics of the American spirit more faithfully illustrated than in the controversy that preceded the Declaration of Independence. The colonists were deeply resentful of measures like the Stamp Act and ill-disposed to tolerate the principle of British interference in American internal affairs. Long years of self-rule had taught them to think of autonomy, not only as a privilege, but as a right; a century and a half of free-living frontier experience had engendered a deep libertarian bias and a hyper-sensitive dread of tyranny. Many of them felt, rightly or wrongly, that the practical advantages of union with England were not enough to compensate them for any substantial diminution of political and economic freedom. Their instinct therefore was to protest and even resist the British "depredations," and the Stamp Act Congress of 1765 resolved that the hated tax had a "manifest tendency to subvert the rights and liberties of the colonists." The British ministry were willing enough to repeal the Stamp Act itself, and they did so. But England could not accept the colonial insistence that Parliament lacked the *power* to impose such exactions on America if it chose to, and in 1766 the "Declaratory Act" was passed, reasserting the doctrine of parliamentary supremacy. Since this was the very doctrine which the liberty-minded colonists could not accede to, the conflict of viewpoints would appear on its face to have been irreconcilable.

A more radically logical people might have concluded at once that the only course open was the highway of revolution. But the past of the colonists, while teaching them to love liberty, had also bequeathed them a solid veneration for the rule of law, a veneration all the greater perhaps because the yoke of the law had always rested so lightly on their shoulders. They desired liberty, which they felt was their moral due; but with almost equal fervor they desired to behave legally. The assertion of parliamentary supremacy loomed as a threat to one or the other of these American ideals; it appeared that a choice must be made between them.

Characteristically, however, America elected to evade that choice, and colonial polemicists began to insist that their opposition to British claims was *both* libertarian and legalistic, that in law as well as in morality Parliament had exceeded its powers. The search for precedent to buttress this argument kept many an American lamp burning for long hours and provides us with an early and excellent example of the creative legalism that was to play such a significant part in the later history of the American nation. The colonists, like good lawyers the world over, piled their arguments on top of one another on the sound theory that if one did not suffice the next might. They argued that the charters, which provided the frames of government for the colonies, had been granted to them by the king, and that they were subject only to the will of His Majesty. Parliament, they said, had no authority to encroach on the charter rights which the king had bestowed. As Alexander Hamilton put it in 1774:

Our charters, the express conditions on which our progenitors relinquished their native countries and came to settle in this, preclude every claim of ruling and taxing us without our assent.

Moreover, said the colonists, even if the charters did not

preclude this parliamentary interference, the British constitution would, since taxation without consent is a violation of natural law and natural law is a premise of the British consitution. Here was a truly remarkable synthesis of philosophy and law, of desire and reason. The natural rights concepts of the Whig philosopher, John Locke, had sunk deep into the consciousness of thoughtful Americans and, indeed, they had found his theories even more persuasive than had their British cousins. The natural order Locke described bore a plausible resemblance to the environment they saw around them; the social contract based on consent which he postulated seemed borne out by their experience with such agreements as the Mayflower Compact and the Fundamental Orders of Connecticut. Now they sought to implement these philosophic generalities further by grafting them on to the British constitution. And far-reaching though this proposition was, the colonists extended it even farther by insisting that a parliamentary act against these principles (now transmuted into *constitutional* principles) was invalid. James Otis, a Massachusetts lawyer trained in the Whig tradition, had flatly said, as early as 1761, that a parliamentary act contrary to the constitution was void, thus refurbishing for American use the venerable English dogma that the common law is above the statute law. And in a pamphlet written against the Stamp Act Otis clarified the implications of this position. After setting forth the natural law doctrine that government can take property only from those who have consented to the government, he said: "These are the first principles of law and justice, and the great barriers of a free state, and of the British constitution in particular." Since the colonists were unrepresented in Parliament, it followed that Parliament had no right, either moral or legal, to tax them.

Furthermore, the colonists went on, Parliament is not only behaving illegally when it taxes us; it is behaving illegally when it seeks to govern our internal concerns in any way, because our allegiance is to the king alone. Here the Americans developed a theory of the relationship between dependencies and the mother country that is strikingly similar to the theory of the modern British Commonwealth of Nations. Among others, James Wilson, one of the most learned of revolutionary statesmen and later a Justice of the United States Supreme Court, undertook to show that this position was supported by the traditions of English constitutional law, and was able to marshal a fairly impressive array of precedents to document his contention.

Whether these dicta were technically sound, whether they would withstand rigorous examination as legal principles—this matters very little in the light of subsequent events. What does matter about these arguments is that the colonists felt compelled to make them and that they were advanced earnestly and repeatedly and never really abandoned. For the colonists these legalistic polemics had the greatest significance, because they seemed to provide a link between their traditional and conservative devotion to the rule of law and their instinctive thrust toward liberty. There were men in the colonies who would have been willing to forego legality in order to achieve separation; and there were others who would have sacrificed liberty in the name of fealty to the mother country. But the majority of thinking men in America wanted both freedom and legality, and they moved toward revolution with the greatest reluctance, stopping constantly to reassure themselves that they were not revolutionists after all. They thought of themselves not as mutineers, but as sober and reasonable defenders of traditional freedom. If they were bent on a revolutionary course, it would be, they felt, a revolution by due process of law. And characteristically, they could see no reason for believing that these objectives were incompatible.

However, as relations with England steadily worsened during the 1770's, the colonists found it increasingly difficult to maintain a moderate stand: the logic of history swept them inexorably toward the Declaration of Independence. It was hard for these men to reconcile themselves to the necessity for such an act, hard for them to relinquish the idea that legal suasion would ultimately win the day. But the intransigence of the English ministry was a stubborn fact, and the colonists gradually came alive to its implication—that only an appeal to arms would answer their purpose. Even then they might have held back, seeking as always to have the best of both worlds. But their own arguments had fanned the flame of a spirit that could not easily be quelled: the doctrine of popular sovereignty was now abroad in the land and clamoring for expression. The colonial legal disquisitions had been premised, almost without exception, on the dogma of popular consent, and it was not easy to hold such a principle within its sober, legalistic framework. The people of America began to insist that the premise be carried to its conclusion, and since Britain refused to concede home rule, that conclusion was plainly revolutionary. And discordantly though the word "revolution" sounded in the ears of such men as Dickinson and Wilson and Hamilton, they were to some degree theoretically disarmed against it by their own postulates.

This spirit of popular revolt, this straight-line drive toward the revolutionary objective, was stimulated and largely symbolized by a recent arrival on American shores, Thomas Paine, whom we have already mentioned. The son of a Norfolk corset-maker, Paine's career had been completely undistinguished before he landed in the New World late in 1774. But somehow in the course of his 37 years he had learned to write the English language with a vividness and clarity that were to mark him as one of the world's great pamphleteers; and somewhere he had acquired a rebellious and unorthodox temperament that made him impatient for change and eagerly willing to press a position to its natural conclusion. These qualities fitted him admirably for the role he was assigned at this crucial juncture in American history. In an attempt to punish Massachusetts for rebellious incidents like the "Boston Tea Party," Parliament had passed certain punitive legislation and in an attempt to enforce it had, in April of 1775, sent troops to Lexington and Concord, where armed resistance was encountered. The following month, the colonists called a Continental Congress to consider retaliatory measures and, although the sentiment in favor of outright separation from England was plainly growing, this convocation was still ruled by moderate counsels and capped its deliberations by reaffirming the allegiance of the Americans to King George. His Majesty responded by declaring officially that the colonies were in a state of rebellion. In retrospect, it seems hard to believe that Americans could, in the face of this royal declaration, continue to resist the movement for separation, but it required a bombshell to dislodge them from their position of hesitant moderation. That bombshell was supplied by Thomas Paine, who published *Common Sense* in January, 1776.

For Paine, the problem that had been vexing America was simply solved. Government, he said, is based on no other justification than the freedom and security of the governed. British rule over America offered the colonists neither freedom nor security, but only tyranny and exactions; therefore, America should renounce allegiance to "the royal brute" of Great Britain and should go her own way. It was an unqualified appeal to the principle of self-interest, to the principle of popular sovereignty, rejecting as fatuous all the sentimental ties that had so far bound America to the crown. And the effect of the pamphlet was electric. Printing presses ran night and day to supply the popular demand; at least 300,000 copies were sold; in the next six months nearly every adult in the colonies had read *Common Sense* or heard it read to him. Everywhere it converted its readers to the cause of independence. It produced almost overnight a wave of antimonarchical feeling that was not to abate until the question of monarchy had become academic in America. It tore away the fabric of veneration toward the motherland that had existed for more than a century. When the smoke had cleared it was evident that the popular will in America was at last firmly set on a revolutionary course.

Paine undoubtedly kindled the spark that led finally to outright rebellion and separation. His contempt for tradition, his straightforward appeal to the unadorned principle of popular sovereignty, his lack of concern for the legal tortuosities that had preoccupied the colonists, had a refreshing and revitalizing effect on the American mind. But this is not to say that the spirit of America was remodeled in the image of Tom Paine. Paine taught the colonists where their interests lay, and his fiery prose gave a powerful stimulus to the movement for popular sovereignty. The doctrine of popular consent was henceforward unchallengeable in America. But Americans nevertheless did not interpret that doctrine in strict, simplistic terms such as Paine's. Even when they had accepted the need for revolution they clung to their old affection for traditionalism and legality, and when the Declaration of Independence came it took a form that reflected both the libertarian and the traditionalistic elements of the American character. It was an appeal to a "candid world," pregnant with the philosophic generalities inherited from Harrington and Locke, explicitly resting on the will of the people. But underneath this radical, philosophic surface an alert observer can trace the outlines of the familiar legal arguments as well. Americans had not abandoned their insistence that the colonial cause was legally defensible; they had simply added the premise that it was philosophically defensible, too. They had not subordinated tradition to a single-minded insistence on popular sovereignty; they had merely learned to contend that tradition ratified the decisions of the popular will.

II. THE ADOPTION OF THE DOCUMENTS

1. The Declaration of Independence

On June 7, 1776, Richard Henry Lee of Virginia, acting under instructions from the Virginia Assembly, offered to the Continental Congress a resolution for independence. Even at this late stage, with commercial intercourse between England

and America interdicted and the clash of arms resounding along the eastern seaboard, the opposition to separation was still substantial. Delegates from six of the colonies had been specifically instructed by their legislatures to oppose a motion for independence, and a fierce debate developed with John Dickinson, supported by James Wilson and others, leading the opposition. On June 10, the debate was recessed for three weeks so that the delegates could return to their states for new instructions. Meantime, a committee was designated to draw up a "Declaration of Independence," so as to have it ready in case the final decision in favor of separation was made. The committee consisted of Benjamin Franklin, John Adams, Roger Sherman, Robert Livingston and Thomas Jefferson, who was made chairman. Its members discussed the general character of the appeal that should be produced and then asked Jefferson to compose it. In two days Jefferson had completed the task; on July 2, the Congress voted to pass Lee's resolution of independence and on July 4, the Declaration itself was issued to "a candid world."

The document that issued from Jefferson's felicitous pen was a mirror of the contemporary American spirit. In later years Jefferson himself said that he had simply been trying "to place before mankind the common sense of the subject in terms so plain and firm as to command their assent . . . it was intended to be an expression of the American mind." And that is indeed what it was. Its list of grievances was a recapitulation of the controversies of the preceding decade; its basic premises were a compound of popular political philosophy and concrete American experience.

What were these premises? First, there was the concept of natural law as the fundamental basis for the rights asserted, a concept implicit in Jefferson's invocation of "the laws of nature and of Nature's God." To Jefferson and his like-minded contemporaries there was nothing strange in the assertion that the truths of the Declaration were "self-evident." The ancient and essentially ethical tradition of natural law, stemming from Cicero and his predecessors, had merged in American thought with the modern Newtonian conception of a universe subject to the "laws" of physics; and it therefore seemed reasonable that the laws of the moral world, like those of the physical world, would be revealed to him who looked closely at the book of nature. In their own experience Americans felt they could see this proposition verified; the natural order of Locke's philosophy seemed, as we have suggested above, a reasonable facsimile of the environment they had come to know and take for granted until the British ministry had disturbed it. It was easy for them to believe that this familiar state of affairs was the *natural* state of affairs; indeed it would have been difficult for them to believe otherwise. And this being the natural condition of man, it followed, they thought, that it was the *moral* condition of man, thus accomplishing a transition from the empirical to the normative which was a commonplace of the eighteenth century, however tantalizingly illogical it may seem to a later generation.

With this concept of the natural order as a starting point, the other "self-evident" truths of the Declaration fell in line like well-trained guardsmen. For one thing, it is apparent that all men are created equal in the state of nature. This assertion was to be sharply criticized from time to time in succeeding years and to be misunderstood even more often. Critics took it to mean that men are equal in physical and mental endowment, a patent absurdity; and not a few simple-minded populists of a later day extracted from it the inference that one man's opinion on any subject is as good as the next man's, that the recognition of distinctions between learning and ignorance, between ability and incompetence is undemocratic. Jefferson and his fellows meant, of course, nothing of the kind. They meant that men were equal in the moral sense and ought to be equal in the political sense. They were drawing on a concept of spiritual equality which was older than Christianity and insisting that the time had come to implement the ideal by erasing legal privileges based on the accident of birth. Again they were aided in reaching this point by the circumstance that the principle of equality was already rooted in their experience. On the frontier, which lay only a few short miles from the doors of even urban Americans, artificial distinctions between men tended to dissolve in the common struggle for subsistence.

Secondly, it is self-evident that men are endowed with the unalienable right to "life, liberty, and the pursuit of happiness." Again, as with all of this, it is only necessary to turn to Locke to find the point of reference. Jefferson later said that when he wrote the Declaration he referred to no book, not even Locke's *Second Treatise*, and this fact is a measure of that book's influence on him and his contemporaries. The ideas, and even the phrases of Locke had become so deeply imbedded in the thinking of educated Americans of the period that they came to mind unbidden. Even Jefferson's use of "the pursuit of happiness" as the third term in the triumvirate of basic rights, instead of Locke's term "estate," [1] was not, as has been pointed out above, necessarily a departure in meaning. Stylistically, "pursuit of happiness" is unquestionably better, and it may have been no more than an instinct for a graceful phrase that caused the substitution.

From here on the philosophy of the Declaration follows the classic eighteenth-century line. Since these rights cannot be maintained in practice without social organization, men agree by social compact to establish a government to secure them. Thus the principle of popular consent is introduced. Since this consent-based government has no justification beyond the protection of rights, it follows that consent must be withdrawn if the government fails to defend the rights of the governed. So the "right of revolution" is reasserted. It remains then merely to demonstrate in a catalog of grievances that George III and his government have left basic rights unprotected and have even taken positive action to encroach on them. And the argumentative circle is complete; the moral warrant for the revolution is indisputably plain.

This then was the Declaration of Independence; this was the "Spirit of '76." At first glance it might seem that it was

[1] See above, p. xi.

merely a reiteration in somewhat more stately language of the arguments of Thomas Paine, it might appear that there was no difference between this spirit and that expressed in the French Declaration of the Rights of Man a few years later. But there were differences, and if they consisted only of variant emphases, they were nevertheless profoundly important. When Paine was defending the French Revolution against Burke in later years he used a phrase which reveals his own attitude and underlines the American outlook by contrast: "That which a whole nation chooses to do," said Paine, "it has a right to do." [2] Whether Paine was willing to stand on this assertion when a few months had passed and he had seen what the Jacobins chose to do in the name of the national will does not really matter. The point is that Paine's straight-line radicalism, his unconcern for tradition, inevitably led toward a doctrine of absolute popular sovereignty; and while the tradition as the Americans understood it was not inimical to the principle of popular control, it did not supply a warrant for popular despotism. The possible inconsistency involved in the linkage of legal traditionalism and popular sovereignty did not disturb them, or if it did it failed to change their minds. Americans wanted the past *and* the present, prescriptive rights *and* natural rights, constitutionalism *and* democracy. These were the objectives they set before them as they began the long war which was inaugurated by the separation from England.

2. The Articles of Confederation

As A. C. McLaughlin has said, "with the announcement of independence, the problem of imperial organization crossed the ocean." [1] The colonists had disapproved British measures

[2] *Thomas Paine, Common Sense and Other Political Writings,* (Adkins), p. 77.

[1] Andrew C. McLaughlin, *A Constitutional History of the United States* (New York and London: D. Appleton Century Co., Inc., 1935), p. 118.

for governing American external affairs, but it was impossible to avoid the hard fact that external policy still had to be considered. Accordingly, Congress began almost immediately after the Declaration to formulate a plan for conduct of the joint affairs of the colonies. In July, 1777, the Articles of Confederation were submitted to the states and within two years all the states except Maryland had ratified. Maryland withheld her approval until March, 1781, not because of distaste for the general provisions of the Articles, but because her citizens felt that certain western lands claimed by Virginia, Pennsylvania, Massachusetts, New York, and Connecticut should be ceded to the nation.

The form of government established by the Articles of Confederation was not very different from the informal arrangement that had developed during the Revolution. Congress was composed of delegates chosen by each state in whatever manner it might choose, and each state delegation was entitled to one vote. Although such institutions as a separate executive authority and a bicameral legislature were commonplace in the state governments of the day, neither of these characteristic principles of later American constitutional theory was embodied in the Articles. Congress was a single unit; and the "President" provided for in Article IX was merely its presiding officer. Executive power was wielded by various committees, at first appointed on an indiscriminate *ad hoc* basis, but in 1781 to some extent integrated by the establishment of permanent departments of Foreign Affairs, Treasury, War, and Marine. Congress was endowed with the power to make war and peace, to conduct foreign affairs, to regulate the Indian tribes, to coin money, and to establish a post office. A limited judicial function is reflected in the authority of Congress to establish tribunals to deal with interstate disputes and with certain issues of marine law.

The nature of these arrangements suggests that America looked upon the government under the Articles as a sort of diplomatic assembly presiding over a league of otherwise independent states; and this description is confirmed by other provisions of the document. The jealous concern of the states to maintain their separate sovereignty is evinced by the provision specifically reserving the "sovereignty, freedom, and independence" of each state. Various "interstate comity" provisions—insuring the extradition of criminals, granting "full faith and credit" in each state to judicial proceedings in every other state, and denying a state the right to deprive citizens of other states of the "privileges and immunities" it accorded its own citizens—are characteristic of agreements often made between sovereign nations.

Partly because it endured for so short a time, the form of government that emerged from these provisions has often been critized by later historians; yet it was not without merits, both present and potential. It is quite conceivable that the Congressional committees which carried on the executive functions might ultimately have coalesced into a responsible cabinet and that the result might have been a form of parliamentary government. The single-house legislature could quite possibly have evolved into a more efficient body than the modern American Congress. The pervasive concern for state sovereignty can be defended, apart from other considerations, on the ground that it expressed the convictions and prejudices of a nation lately freed from external control and that no more centralized system would for the time being have seemed tolerable. Further advances toward nationhood, it might be argued, could be made gradually as the need became clear. Meantime the condition of the United States was regarded by many contemporaries as sound and healthy; and indeed there is some reason to believe that these friends of the Articles may have been in a majority even at the time of the ratification of the new Federal Constitution.

Nevertheless, although appraisal of the government under the Articles may vary now, as it did then, it is hardly deniable that the system was beset with grave deficiencies, especially from the viewpoint of those who had hoped to see the establishment of a genuine nation. The powers withheld from Congress were far more important than those that were granted.

The states, for example, retained the power to make their own commercial regulations and the national government was not given authority to pass trade regulations for the confederation as a whole. Equally important was the fact that Congress was not delegated the power to levy taxes; in order to obtain funds for carrying on its operations, the national government was dependent upon requisitions against the states.

But important as were these omissions from the catalog of federal powers under the Articles of Confederation, the fatal weakness of the national government was a more general one —that it had no sanctions to enforce the powers that *were* granted to it, or to compel the states to conform to a national pattern. This deficiency is illustrated most dramatically in connection with finance—while the states were in theory bound to supply funds in proportion to the value of surveyed land within their borders, in fact they honored the national government's requisitions when they chose to and breached them when they preferred. Nothing could be done to make the states comply if they were reluctant to do so; actual coercion of the states by the national government was unthinkable even if it had been possible, for the average American thought of himself as a Virginian or a New Yorker first and as an American second. And the central government was equally ill-armed to enforce confederation laws against citizens, mainly because the Articles had failed to provide for a federal judiciary. Adherence to confederation laws was supposed to be enforced by the courts of the states, but these tribunals were subject to no over-riding appellate authority. This meant that they could follow national laws or ignore them, depending on their own preferences.

These faults in the system of government established by the Articles of Confederation were reflected in the history of the period. The debt contracted during the Revolution remained unpaid, and this was felt by the many bourgeois-minded among the colonists to constitute a continuing reproach to national honor. Great Britain discriminated against American merchant ships, and the government of the United States was powerless to retaliate. Within the confederation itself the lack of a uniform currency and the multiplication of trade barriers among the states were a constant handicap to commerce. A shortage of currency in the years following the war put the debtors of the west in difficult straits, and state legislatures were urged to pass measures to relieve them—"stay laws" to postpone the foreclosure of mortgages, "tender acts" which made it obligatory that the creditor accept produce in payment of debts owing to him, and so on.

These developments were viewed with the greatest alarm by a growing body of opinion in the colonies. It might seem— as it did to some—that the carnival of state sovereignty and populist revolt was merely the logical extension of principles laid down in the Revolution, that the several states having broken with England in the name of popular consent were now engaged in reaping the harvest of freedom. But to others the current state of affairs seemed to verge dangerously on anarchy, and they began to fear that the modest aims they had cherished in 1776 were getting out of hand. A group of public-minded—and nationalist-minded—leaders of opinion from various states began to take form, their identity of purpose becoming clearer and clearer as they corresponded with one another and argued against the proponents of the confederation principles. This group included such men as George Washington, the hero of the revolutionary struggle; Alexander Hamilton, Washington's young and brilliant aide-de-camp; James Madison, the thoughtful and scholarly Virginian who was to become known as the "Father of the Constitution"; James Wilson of Pennsylvania, perhaps the greatest legal scholar in the America of his day; Gouverneur Morris of the same state, a statesman of great ability and aristocratic leanings; Elbridge Gerry and Rufus King of Massachusetts; John Rutledge of South Carolina, and Oliver Ellsworth of Connecticut, both of whom were later to be appointed to the Chief Justiceship of the United States Supreme Court. In later years, most of these men took their place in the ranks of what became known as the Federalist Party; some, like Madison and Gerry, were won over to the "Anti-Federalist" party of Jefferson. But for the time being they were commonly devoted to the cause of national union. The Federalists sought a revolution that would break the bonds with the mother country; to that end they had embraced the principle of republicanism as their moral justification. But the revolution they had envisioned was intended to preserve as well as innovate; it was meant to enshrine not only the will of the people but also the sober virtues of the Anglo-American middle class tradition. And now it seemed they were faced with a peril which, as Americans, they deeply dreaded—the peril that one principle might become predominant, that the nation might be forced to choose between the tradition and the people. They faced, or thought they faced, a danger which would be known throughout the world a few years later as "Jacobinism."

Fortunately for the future of American union the faction in the colonies which was most stirred by these fears consisted of those who by heredity and training were the natural leaders of the new nation. Whether or not the nascent democratic movement contained the seeds of Jacobinism, it certainly did constitute a powerful disunionist force, and the conservative leaders of opinion who had helped make the Revolution now set themselves the task of preventing it from realizing these twin potentials. The democratic spirit whose excesses they dreaded was in fact only half-formulated and ill-supplied with men to plead its cause, and the result was that the traditional leaders of the community were able to carry through a successful program for establishing union and mitigating the dangers of unchecked popular rule.

Yet it would be a serious mistake (though it is one frequently made) to interpret the movement for union and the eventual establishment of the National Constitution as a counter-revolution in the profound sense, as a "Thermidorean reaction." So to regard this development is to misunderstand both the nature of the American community of the 1780's and the character of its leaders. The democratic drive that found expression in "stay laws" and "tender acts" was disturbing to the property-conscious merchants of the seaboard, but it fell considerably short of wild, irresponsible mob rule; from first to last it was moderated by the essential conservatism of the American temperament. Moreover, the proponents of a new constitution to establish national union never undertook to controvert the Revolution's central principle—the consent of the governed. They had embraced that principle in the course of the struggle with England and they had no thought of abandoning it, but only to see that in the working out it did not become self-destructive. Their aim, in short, was not to defeat the Revolution, but to realize its objectives as they understood them, and it was with that end in mind that they inaugurated the movement which culminated in the Convention at Philadelphia in 1787.[2]

As has already been suggested, the success of this movement can be attributed in part to the fact that it was supported by the men who were the community's accepted leaders. This superiority of personnel is apparent from the beginning to the end of the constitutional movement. In the closing years of the Confederation a veritable flood of correspondence coursed between men like Washington, Hamilton, Madison, Pendleton, Jay, Randolph, and Knox laying the groundwork for the ultimate assembly at Philadelphia. Thus was added to their natural prestige of leadership a communion of purpose which immeasurably augmented the enterprise's prospects of success.

3. The Constitution

A number of traditional clichés have been used to describe the Convention of 1787 and the document it produced, and among these perhaps the most persistent is the statement that the Constitution was a "bundle of compromises." Like most such standard descriptions, this one obscures almost as much as it clarifies, yet it does furnish a taking-off point for un-

[2] Cf. the Resolution of Congress of February 21, 1787, to convene a national Convention "for the sole and express purpose of revising the Articles of Confederation," reprinted on p. 23.

derstanding the work of the Convention. The most important compromise from the viewpoint of those who attended the Convention was the agreement as to the method for choosing the House of Representatives and the Senate, the two legislative bodies of the proposed government. The delegation from Virginia had come to the Convention armed with a plan which had probably been drafted by James Madison.[1] This plan was startlingly radical: it ignored the assumption that the delegates were assembled to consider revisions to the Articles of Confederation, and boldly set forth an entirely new structure of government; that suggested government was frankly nationalistic, sharply in contrast to the loose confederation of the past. No doubt, the Virginia proposal was a part of the program of the advocates of unionism, a calculated attempt to dislodge the principle of states' rights at the outset, and to some extent it accomplished its purpose. Those who might have hesitated to depart from the decentralization of the Articles were comforted when they did so by the reflection that the Virginia Plan would have gone much farther. But the Virginia proposal also raised one of the bitterest issues of the convention, since it provided that both Houses of Congress be chosen on the basis of population. This would mean that a few large states, among them of course Virginia itself, would enjoy a commanding voice in the new government, and the smaller states objected strenuously. They countered with the New Jersey Plan,[2] a much more modest proposal for revising the Articles, which would have preserved the autonomy of the states as the basic principle of the new system, and for a time the Convention deadlocked on this issue. The final compromise—the "Great Compromise"—was to give the states equal representation in the Senate while retaining the principle of representation by population in the

---

[1] Although the plan was officially submitted to the Convention by Randolph. Cf. both "The Virginia Plan as Offered by Randolph" and "The Virginia Plan as Reported by the Committee of the Whole," reprinted on pp. 24ff.

[2] Cf. pp. 30ff.

House. This meant that the smaller states would retain the power to defend themselves against a possible coalition of their more populous neighbors, and the compromise is of course historically important because it saved the Convention. But its importance to this analysis is chiefly in that it illustrates the comparative triviality of the issues on which the delegates divided. As history was to demonstrate, there was no realistic ground for believing that the large states would make common cause against the small; the great controversies in American politics have arisen out of sectional and economic rivalries which have grouped both small and large states together on opposing sides. The provision for equal representation in the Senate was later to assume great importance, since it enabled the South to protect its interests against the more populous north; but the idea that the large states as such would conspire to oppress the small was without foundation. It is significant that this most troublesome of the convention's problems was to a large degree imaginary.

Something of the same sort can be said about the other major compromises. Contention arose over the question of how slaves should be counted in setting up a base for representation in the House of Representatives and for direct taxation. Ideally the South, whose slave population was already large, would have preferred to count slaves as persons for purposes of representation and not to count them as property for purpose of taxation, but the northern delegates were not enthusiastic about this congenial arrangement. The Convention resolved the disagreement by adopting the "three-fifths" clause of Article I, Section 2, Paragraph 3, which provided that each slave should count as three-fifths of a person, both for purposes of representation and direct taxation. In later years, slavery became such a fierce issue in America that this compromise appeared very important, but in fact its importance was not widely recognized at the time. It can hardly be said to reflect a vital conflict in contemporary American opinion.

Two other compromises are traditionally emphasized in discussing the work of the Convention—the agreement that

Congress would not use the commerce power to interfere with the importation of slaves until 1808 (Article I, Section 9); and the agreement for choosing the President by electoral vote in the first instance and by individual vote of the states if no candidate receives a majority (Article II, Section 1). Since the first of these became of historical interest only in 1808 and since, as far as the second is concerned, the rise of political parties made it almost academic, neither of these compromises can be regarded as involving issues of very great moment. The conclusion seems inescapable that the controversies of the Convention were comparatively trivial in their main concerns.

When we turn to consider the matters over which controversy did *not* rage, the explanation of this fact becomes apparent. When we enumerate the issues on which there was no need to compromise because there was little or no substantial disagreement, the real nature of the constitutional movement becomes plain. The startling fact is that the Convention was in almost solid agreement on the basic presumptions of political science which were to form the cornerstones of the new constitutional structure, and their concord on these presumptions was far more significant than their disagreements on the matters that led to the compromises. To begin with, the delegates assumed from the first that the form of the government would be republican, by which they meant that it would find its great source of power in the people. Some of the delegates, as has been suggested, wished to see democracy controlled; some were inordinately fearful of majority tyranny and distrustful of popular judgments. This was certainly the attitude of Hamilton and Gouverneur Morris, two of the ablest and most vocal delegates, and it was shared in varying degrees by such members as William Randolph of Virginia and Elbridge Gerry of Massachusetts. All of the states at this time imposed some restrictions on the right of suffrage, and most of them required a property qualification for voting. There is no doubt that many of the Convention's delegates would have been pleased to see such restrictions embodied in the Federal Constitution and were deterred mainly by the fear that an attempt to prescribe a uniform standard would imperil ratification. But hardly any would propose an outright retreat from the revolutionary principle of popular consent, and no such course of action was even considered by the Convention.

In the second place, the Convention was in no serious disagreement about the institution of separation of powers, together with the concomitant idea of checks and balances. Governmental power, they agreed, should be divided between three branches of government—the legislative, the executive, and the judicial. Each branch was to be independent of the other, and this separateness of identity was to be preserved, in the case of the Congress and the Presidency by providing for distinct methods of election, and in the case of the judiciary by providing that the judges would hold office for life "during good behavior." At the same time, each branch was to be armed with certain powers to check the encroachments of the others. The presidential veto power, for example, would enable the chief executive to forestall legislation he disapproved; the participation of the Senate in appointments and treaty-making and the control over appropriations by the whole Congress would prevent executive excesses; and the authority of the courts to refuse enforcement of an unconstitutional law would make it possible for that branch to defend itself. The result—in theory—was a balanced and moderate government which would be unlikely to develop into a tyranny because it was divided against itself. The delegates were prepared to risk the danger that the government would have the faults of its virtues—that it might prove cumbersome and slow to act when the need for swift decision arose. This was the form of government they were used to. Americans had seen the principle of the separation of powers in operation for many years in colonial governments where the governor had acted as the representative of the king or proprietor while the assembly represented the colonists. They had embodied the principle in the state constitutions they drew up following the separation from England. Those who were theoretically inclined had found confirmation for their bias in favor of separation of powers in the writings of Montesquieu and in those of their own John Adams and Thomas Jefferson. By 1787, the principle was an axiom beyond serious dispute in America, and it would have been quite unthinkable to present a frame of government which did not divide the executive from the legislative, and both from the judicial powers.

Nor was there need to compromise on the question as to whether the new Constitution was to be "the supreme law of the land." As has been suggested above, the most serious defect of the Articles of Confederation had been their failure to provide the central government with a means for enforcing its commands. The result was that the national government was in practice inferior to the member states even as to the purposes of the union. Now the Convention, with very little argument, took the all-important steps of asserting the supremacy of the national government and its laws (Article VI, Section 2) and of providing a means—the Federal judiciary —by which that supremacy could be implemented by enforcing the national commands against individuals. It is impossible to exaggerate the significance of this dual innovation. The supremacy clause has been called "the linchpin of the Constitution," and it is indeed hard to imagine that a national government could have been established without it. The authority to act directly on individuals in collecting taxes and enforcing laws was a new departure in the practice of federalism. Yet neither of these advances gave rise to serious controversy within the Convention hall.

The basic agreement among the delegates was even more striking when they turned to consider those sections of the Constitution that had most directly to do with property rights and commercial relations. As has already been suggested, there was at the time a fairly clear-cut split between the interests of land-holding debtors on the one hand and merchant creditors on the other; the former group had been inclined to advocate "soft" money and a relaxation of creditors' rights. But no such division of opinion was apparent among the members of the Convention. The delegates seemed to be unanimously agreed that a primary object of the new government was to prevent further state attacks on property, and when proposals to accomplish this end were brought before them, the members handled them in short order. The issuance of paper money by the states was absolutely prohibited as was the passage of "tender laws"; the states were forbidden to enact laws "impairing the obligation of contracts." And in spite of the fact that these three provisions were aimed directly at the policies advocated by substantial factions in several of the states, they were accepted by the Convention almost without discussion.

Evidently then the members of the Convention were a remarkably like-minded group who agreed, by and large, on such fundamental issues as republicanism, separation of powers, and the idea of constitutionalism itself. These ideas were, as we have seen above, so deeply rooted in the American heritage that it was out of the question to propose a frame of government which did not embody them. But beyond that the delegates were generally in accord on certain questions which were not regarded as quite so axiomatic by the American people as a whole—that the new government should be strengthened as to its powers and as to its relationships with the states; that it should be given the authority to act directly on individuals; that its laws within its sphere should be indisputably supreme; that the states should be curbed in their tendencies to impinge on the rights of property-holders. How can we account for this impressive concord in the Convention when we reflect that the nation it presumably represented was sharply divided on these very points?

The answer is not very far to seek. The members of the Convention were in agreement because they represented in very heavy preponderance a particular opinion group, or class, of the American populace; the Philadelphia gathering was by no stretch of the imagination a cross-section of the nation. It consisted of the same men—or the same kind of men—who had played a major part in carrying through the revolutionary struggle: a sober, serious, property-conscious, well-informed, even scholarly minority. These men knew what they wanted when they essayed the task of constitution-making, just as they had known what they wanted when they donned the garb of revolutionaries. They had wanted (remarkable conception!) a "moderate revolution" whose moral justification would be found both in the will of the people and in the constitutional tradition, a revolution which would disturb the status quo only so much as they felt it ought to be disturbed. Reckless of strict logic, pragmatic to the core, they had incorporated in their revolutionary ideology the most disparate principles, secure in the confidence that they could make the best of half-a-dozen different worlds. Now they were implementing that confidence still further and piling new paradoxes on the American political complex. The constitution they had created was, with all its checks and balances, certain to become the instrument of majority rule. Yet the very instrument that drew its power from the people laid down restrictions on the popular will, a result which might sound to a logician very much like nonsense. So likewise with the power granted to the central government—on the one hand, it was desired to strengthen it substantially; on the other hand, too strong a government was traditionally dreaded in America. The solution was characteristic: the government was revitalized by granting it broad powers and at the same time weakened by institutionalizing rivalry between its main branches. The separation of powers principle was carefully calculated to prevent a majority from seizing power and using it without restriction. The enumeration of national powers meant that the government, even in the hands of a majority, was denied the right to exercise powers *not* enumerated. Sections nine and ten of Article I were crowded with prohibitions against the national government and the states respectively. And although a formal Bill of Rights was not appended to the original document, the addition of this safeguard against unchecked power (whether in the hands of the majority or not) was approved by most of those who had participated in the Convention. Finally, the most serious question of all at the moment—whether the United States was to be a true nation or a league of sovereign states—was not confronted at all but was set aside for the disposal of history.

The Constitution itself was consistent with either interpretation, as interminable constitutional debates of the future were to show. The nation-confederation problem had been dealt with like all major political questions in America: by embracing both alternatives and trusting to providence that the incompatibility could be permanently ignored. And the men who had fashioned this instrument of government knew that whether the majority of the people seemed at the moment to like the Constitution or not, it would work for them because it so faithfully reflected the American political character.

4. The Ratification

The events that followed the presentation of the finished document to the states demonstrate the validity of the propositions that have permeated this discussion so far. To begin with, in the ratification struggle it became apparent that the people as a whole did not share the Convention's nearly unanimous enthusiasm for a new instrument of government; indeed it is fairly clear that a majority of the populace was opposed to ratification. On the other hand and in the second place, it is equally evident that the people were not opposed to the basic premises of the Constitution's political faith—republicanism, constitutionalism, separation of powers, but were animated chiefly by a somewhat ill-informed suspicion that the new government would encroach on popular liberties. Thirdly, the ratification struggle and its successful conclusion demonstrated that the "Federalists" (those who had spearheaded the movement for a new constitution) still enjoyed a superiority of leadership which enabled them to impose their will on the nation even though the majority disapproved. And finally, the rapid development during the post-ratification period of almost universal veneration for the new organic law suggested that the instrument created in 1787 was, however lacking in logical symmetry, an appropriate frame of government for a nation more concerned with results than with logic.

The struggle over ratification was intense and even bitter, but the most striking thing about it is the comparative impotence of those who opposed the new Constitution. That they were in a majority in most of the states seems plain enough, but their preponderance was purely numerical. Both argumentatively and strategically their opponents enjoyed a clear advantage. By far the most powerful anti-federalistic argument was based on the curious fact that the Convention had failed to include a Bill of Rights in the proposed constitution. Considering the American preoccupation with the concept of fundamental rights discussed above and the standard practice of appending Bills of Rights to the state constitutions this omission stands forth as the one great tactical miscalculation of the Convention. Apparently the delegates thought that a detailed list of limitations on the federal government was unnecessary, since the powers of the government were already restricted by the principle of delegation (this was the concept, implicit in the Constitution and ultimately made explicit in the Tenth Amendment, that the national government could exercise only the powers enumerated in the Constitution, while all other powers were reserved to the states). But this argument—wrong in any case as the history of the "necessary and proper" clause, Article I, Section 8, Paragraph 18, was to show—was too subtle for most voters, and the anti-federalists were able to argue that the omission betrayed an intention to subvert the liberties of the people. Much of the wind was drawn from the sails of this argument, however, when it was agreed that a Bill of Rights along traditional American lines would be added by the first session of Congress under the new government, and in some key states this was made in effect a condition of ratification.

Apart from this issue, the polemical weapons in the anti-federalist arsenal were relatively few and ineffective as compared with those the Federalists were able to bring to bear. One of the most striking things about the *Federalist* papers, written by Hamilton, Madison and Jay for the ratification struggle in New York, is the unanswerability of their arguments in terms of American political presumptions. A Turgot or a Paine might sneer at the elaborate description of the separation of powers in the new Constitution, but few Americans on either side of the ratification argument were disposed to question it. A doctrinaire democrat might point out that the concept of "republicanism" embodied in the proposed governmental system fell somewhat short of the populist ideal, but Americans were not doctrinaire democrats, and the moderate, Madisonian definition of republicanism had a reassuring, familiar ring. A Patrick Henry might be willing to forego all chance of national union in order to insure the continued, unqualified autonomy of Virginia; but most Americans were inclined to feel that things could be so arranged as to achieve the advantages of union without paying its price. As the state conventions called for the purpose of considering ratification ran their course, it became increasingly apparent that the antifederalists were poorly provided with specific objections to the new frame of government, and that they were forced to rest their opposition largely on the vague and general charge that the whole instrument was part of a design to establish centralizing tyranny in America. Such an argument had a powerful appeal to those who were already convinced, but it was not calculated to sway those who were wavering.

Moreover, the strategic forehandedness of the Federalists—their superiority in leadership—often served to carry the day when persuasion would not. In Pennsylvania, ratification was accomplished by political steamroller tactics that left a trail of bitterness in their wake—but it was accomplished. In Massachusetts, the opponents of ratification constituted a majority of the convention, but the ultimate vote went in favor of ratification, largely because the men of influence and cunning were on the other side. Even in Virginia, where the foes of ratification were represented by the most powerful champions, the Federalists outmaneuvered their opponents time after time. The ratification of the Constitution, like its composition, was a tribute to the leadership qualities of the class that had piloted America throughout these first stormy years of her national history.

Ratification having been achieved by the narrowest of margins and against the preferences of what seems to have been a majority in the nation, its aftermath is all the more remarkable. Not all the wounds opened by the ratification struggle were easily healed, and this was especially true of the central issue, the problem of states' rights. The idea of decentralization had been espoused by a faction calling themselves "Anti-Federalists," and it chanced that this group was also in general composed of men who were more sympathetic to popular government than were many of the Federalists. "States' rights" thus became identified in the popular mind with the democratic spirit, and the alliance created vast difficulties in the years to come, since the cause of state sovereignty was able to draw support from the cause of democracy. The Anti-Federalists, hard-up for leaders in the ratification controversy, soon found them in men like Thomas Jefferson, James Madison, George Clinton of New York, and Albert Gallatin of Pennsylvania. As the group around Hamilton demonstrated their predilection in favor of the mercantile interests of the Eastern seaboard, this Jeffersonian faction claimed the allegiance of the landed interests of the South and West, so that states' rights, populism, and agrarianism were forged into a powerful alliance. This triple entente was not only the basis for Jefferson's party (now re-named Republican). It was also the basis of an alignment in American political doctrine that persisted with more or less vitality until the Civil War and, in fact, still revives from time to time in the modern era. Thus the ratification controversy can be said to have set the patterns of American political factionalism for many years to come. But the Constitution itself, the supposed object of contention, was warmly embraced. In a few years, almost in months, the vestiges of opposition to the new Constitution melted away, and the organic law became regarded as above reproach, an American symbol of semi-religious quality. The Anti-Federalists, who had so fiercely opposed ratification, indeed coalesced into the Republican party of Jefferson, but their attacks centered now, not on the Constitution, but on alleged perversions of that sacred document by the Federalist party of Washington and Hamilton. A direct assault on the Constitution itself by a public figure was quite out of the question, in spite of the fact that that instrument had been damned as a conspiracy against freedom a few short years before. Partly this fervent enthusiasm for the document is no doubt to be attributed to the wave of commercial prosperity that followed immediately upon its adoption, little though the Constitution may have had to do with this revival of trade. But there can be small question that the popularity of the instrument must be traced in large part to its peculiar "fitness" for the American political temperament, its effectiveness in reflecting and resolving the problems that were characteristic of the American political scene. In their pragmatic, patchwork way the framers had built very well.

And finally, the enduring quality of both the Constitution and the worship of it by succeeding generations of Americans must be explained in some measure by the artistry of interpretation that was lavished upon it by commentators, by statesmen, and above all by the Justices of the Supreme Court. There is not space here to sketch in any detail the story of the Constitution's growth and development, the elaboration of the legal meaning of its principal clauses. But to ignore the fact that American political thought became very largely a matter of legal construction of the Constitution rather than abstract speculation would be to ignore a central fact about the American political character, and about the Constitution itself. Foreign observers have often remarked that political questions in America have a way of becoming legal questions. The explanation is to be found in the circumstance referred to so often above—that the nation has never been willing to regard its conflicts as irreconcilable, but has proceeded on the assumption that it is possible to ride both horns of most dilemmas. In a world of deep and irresolvable conflicts legalism can have only a limited place, since the questions that divide society transcend the issue of legality. But in a nation which is convinced that inconsistency is tolerable, legalism becomes king. The *ad hoc,* contingent process of judicial exclusion and inclusion is appropriate to cope with a society which has refused to decide that a single principle of politics shall be its central guide and has preferred to embrace several principles indiscriminately.

III. THE DOCUMENTS AS EXPRESSIONS OF POLITICAL IDEAS

The American Commonwealth has come a long way since the days when the thirteen former Colonies gave themselves the Constitution, after adopting the Declaration of Independence. In writing its provisions, the framers were not at all sure how long it would last. At the end of *The Federalist,* David Hume is cited as authority for the risks involved in constitution-making:

To balance a large state or society on general laws (meaning a constitution) is a work of so great difficulty, that no human genius, however comprehensive, is able, by the mere dint of reason and reflection to effect it. The judgments of many must unite in the work; experience must guide their labor; time must bring it to perfection, and the feeling of inconveniences must correct the mistakes which they *inevitably* fall into in their first trials and experiments.[1]

If anyone had shown them a vision of the United States in the twentieth century, they would have been surprised and

[1] Italics Hamilton's; cf. *The Federalist,* No. 85 (New York: Putnam, 1888), p. 551.

yet they would also have been profoundly satisfied. The technical progress, the extraordinary material welfare would no doubt startle them; but the political stability would seem to them welcome testimony to the soundness of their political principles, and the world-wide sway would confirm them in their faith in progress and the gradual improvement of the human race. But what would no doubt perplex them beyond measure would be to discover that the American of today had become doubtful of both the principles and the progress, and that somehow the very success of the enterprise which they had set on foot seemed to fill their descendants with hesitation, if not with downright skepticism. Carl Becker surely would have startled them when he commented:

What seems but common sense in one age, often seems but nonsense in another. Such for the most part is the fate which has overtaken the sublime truths enshrined in the Declaration of Independence.[2]

One could easily extend this argument. It raises the question as to what is living and what is dead of the political ideas embodied in the documents here under consideration.

1. The Role of the Documents in Subsequent American History

We can, of course, only sketch certain broad outlines here. Although the Declaration of Independence and the Constitution were related in that they both expressed, as we have seen, the American political character, there can be no doubt that they differed profoundly in their emphasis. The Declaration was, after all, a fervent outpouring of the libertarian spirit, a revolutionary document; the Constitution was chiefly concerned, on the other hand, with the problem of ordering the freedoms the Revolution had won. That there should be a certain conflict between them was therefore perhaps inev-

[2] Becker, *op. cit.*, p. 233.

itable, and there have been times when it seemed that the contrast in their aims made them basically incompatible.

So it appeared for example to the old-line proponents of states' rights in the early years of the nineteenth century when the Supreme Court under the Chief Justiceship of the great John Marshall bent itself to the task of welding the young republic into a true nation. Marshall asserted and maintained the supremacy of the national court over the courts of the states when federal questions were involved; he upheld such national legislation as the act incorporating the Bank of the United States, in spite of the charge that Congress had here exceeded its constitutional powers; and he struck down state laws which threatened to fragmentize the national structure. To advocates of states' rights like John Randolph of Roanoke and John Taylor of Caroline these *dicta* represented a darkly ominous threat to liberty, and Randolph was moved to say:

if, with the most approved spring lancets, you draw the last drop of blood from our veins; if, *secundum artem,* you draw the last shilling from our pockets, what are the checks of the Constitution to us? A fig for the Constitution! When the scorpion's sting is probing us to the quick, shall we stop to chop logic? [1]

Nevertheless, the views of the Chief Justice prevailed; the cause of national union was greatly fortified by Marshall's forthright pronouncements. And, as time wore on, more and more Americans began to feel that the choice Randolph and Taylor had propounded between liberty and union was a false one and that the proper course for the United States was that suggested by a famous peroration of Daniel Webster: "Liberty *and* Union, now and forever, one and inseparable!" [2] In short, it was felt, at least in the North, that the old equation of freedom with state autonomy was a false one and that

[1] Henry Adams, *John Randolph,* ed. John T. Morse, Jr. (Boston: Houghton, Mifflin & Co., 1896), p. 279.

[2] *Selected Speeches of Daniel Webster,* Preface and Introduction by A. J. George (Boston: D. C. Heath & Co., 1911), p. 234.

the principles of the Declaration would be realized in practice only if they were supported by a sound democratic nationalism.

But this new solution was not to pass into the structure of American constitutionalism unchallenged. The issue of states' rights had been, as we have seen, among those left in a suspended state by the Convention, and no court, not even one directed by the genius of Marshall, could give a conclusive answer to the question the delegates had feared to confront. And this became all the more true when the states' rights viewpoint became conjoined with a second great unresolved problem—that of chattel slavery. The conjunction of the two was in some ways a historical coincidence: the North, where slavery was economically unfeasible, also became in the first few decades of the nineteenth century far more populous than the South, and Northern statesmen became naturally enough the spokesmen of unionism, since the consolidated Union they envisioned was one they would control. The South, on the other hand, was apprehensive that the growing Northern majority would use the power of a centralized government to strike at slavery which was now regarded as essential to the survival of Southern civilization; and the leaders of "the Cotton Kingdom" therefore clung to and refurbished the states' rights doctrine.[3] It was an occasion of the most extreme difficulty and complexity, with Southerners insisting that the American libertarian tradition enshrined the right of a state to keep thousands of human beings in the legal status of cattle, and Northerners arguing that the sacred cause of union and liberty justified them in taxing the South so as to preserve the existence and profits of New England manufactur-

[3] The states' rights doctrine as a defense of the South against interference from the northern States found its foremost spokesman later in John C. Calhoun (1782-1850), who at one time advocated secession from the Union rather than compliance with federal laws. His major works are: *A Disquisition on Government* and *A Discourse on the Constitution and Government of the United States.* (The former is reprinted in "The American Heritage Series, No. 10, [New York: The Liberal Arts Press, Inc.]).

ers. Out of this welter of idealism and casuistry only one fact really emerged clearly: that the American Constitution was face to face with its severest test. For once the traditional American faith that conflicts would resolve themselves within the structure of constitutionalism was proved groundless, and it took the bitter and bloody Civil War to establish beyond further argument that chattel slavery would go and the union would survive.

The Northern victory made it clear, as the Constitution had not, that the American nation was in the phrase of Chief Justice Chase "an indestructible union of indestructible states." But the triumph of the North was also the triumph of industrialism, and the problem of conflict between the Declaration and the Constitution soon presented itself in a new guise. In the hands of a business-minded Supreme Court, the Constitution was converted in the later years of the nineteenth century into a charter of economic rights for corporate enterprise, and with the help of the "due process clause" of the Fourteenth and Fifth Amendments and the "commerce clause" of Article I, the federal judges frustrated reformist efforts to clear the way for "pursuit of happiness" which the Declaration had promised. Meanwhile the protection of Negro rights which the North had attempted to insure through the passage of the Thirteenth, Fourteenth and Fifteenth Amendments was minimized by judicial decision.

But in the 1930's the course of constitutional interpretation underwent still another change. The Fourteenth Amendment ceased being used by the Court to stifle economic experimentation and became instead a guarantee of individual freedoms such as speech, press, and a fair trial against action by the states; and the commerce clause became, as it had been for Marshall, a grant of power to the national government rather than a limitation. With these developments it might be said that the Declaration and the Constitution moved closer together than they had even been before. The inevitable gap between ideal and working system still existed to underline the fact that the source of a model political order is to be

found, not in a frame of government, but in the spirit of the people who direct it. Nevertheless, it was plain now that the American constitutional framework was to be conceived, not as a barrier but as a bridge to the ultimate realization of the Declaration's ideals.

2. The Role of the Documents in the World at Large

The breadth of the Constitution's theoretical base, including its compromises and contradictions, has enabled it to play a considerable role in shaping constitutional thought and practice everywhere. To be sure, no major European state has adopted the pattern of the American organization as such. But constitutionalism, federalism, the separation of powers and the bill of rights all have become standard aspects of constitutional thought in Europe and throughout the world. And wherever men have gathered to consider drafting a constitution, they have studied American constitutional theory and practice.

When the Dominions of Canada, of Australia and of South Africa came to build their constitutional structures, the American experience, especially in the field of federalism, was of great importance to them, as it has been to some extent since that time. Their governmental structure is a combination of British and American patterns; the two flowing from a common ideological source have been reunited, as it were, in these effectively operating federations.

When the Swiss came to revise their ancient confederal structure, they turned to America for guidance, and the constitution of 1848 bears the mark of this process. When the ill-fated Frankfurt parliament tried to unite Germany in peace and freedom, the leading spirits were constantly discussing their problems in terms of the American precedent. In the efforts after the second world war to reconstitute and reconstruct the democratic basis of constitutional life in France, in Italy, and finally in Germany, the Constitution of the United States provided a loadstar. We find striking influences

in the field of federalism, of judicial review and other items, especially in the field of human rights. Finally and still more recently, the drafters of a constitution for a European Community have utilized extensively the experience of the United States as a measuring rod by which to test their own plans and proposals.

The demonstrative and educational value of the Declaration of Independence and of the Constitution results, however, from an indirect influence upon constitutional developments which were local and autonomous. But there is a wider arena in which the constitutional tradition of the United States has achieved world significance. When President Wilson set forth the plan for a League of Nations—a plan which was nurtured by a group of private organizations deeply imbued with this tradition—he actually projected onto the world plane the thinking which had been embodied in America's constitutional documents. The fact that the League failed has dimmed the vision which animated its builders. Characteristically, its constitution was called a covenant. It was in the tradition of republicanism and constitutionalism as cherished at the time of the American revolution. This is not the place to explore the reasons for its failure. The establishment of the United Nations proved this failure to be a temporary one, anyhow. For the United Nations is another and perhaps a more vigorous sprout from the same root. It, too, is in line with the basic core of constitutionalism. Its Declaration of Universal Human Rights while at present neither enforced nor enforceable clearly demonstrates the forward march of the inherent ideas. Nor should we be unduly concerned about the temporary unenforceability; have previous bills of right been fully or even approximately enforced? The United States has been at work for over a century and a half trying to make its bill of rights work; great strides have been made; but the ideal is far from being a reality.

Precisely because there culminate in these great American documents trends which the accumulated dross of European government and privileged status would not allow to come to

grips with reality, they were eventually able to challenge Europe and the European order of things. They were able to provide the framework for such halting efforts at a universal order under law as the League of Nations and the United Nations have been able to institutionalize. In doing so the United States has been fulfilling the hopes expressed by Immanuel Kant, ardent partisan that he was of the constitutional federation of all free nations. It seemed like a utopia in his day. He admitted as much. But anticipating the role of the United States in establishing a universal constitutional order he added:

For, if Fortune ordains that a powerful and enlightened people should form a republic—which by its very nature is inclined to perpetual peace—this would serve as a center of federal union for other states wishing to join, and thus secure conditions of freedom among the states in accordance with the idea of the law of nations. Gradually, through different unions of this kind, the federation would extend further and further.[1]

This sentence written a few years after the American Revolution by a philosopher who applauded the American constitutional enterprise pointed the way that the ideas of American constitutionalism have gone since they were first definitely formulated in the documents here presented.

[1] Kant, *Perpetual Peace*, trans. M. Campbell Smith, edited by A. Robert Caponigri (The Library of Liberal Arts," No. 3, [New York: The Liberal Arts Press, Inc., 1948]), p. 17.

SELECTED BIBLIOGRAPHY

Adams, R. G., *Political Ideas of the American Revolution,* Durham, 1922.

Becker, Carl L., *The Declaration of Independence,* New York, 1942.

—— *The Heavenly City of the Eighteenth-Century Philosophers,* New Haven, 1932.

Bury, J. B., *The Idea of Progress,* London, 1920.

Corwin, Edward S., *The Constitution and What it Means Today,* Princeton, 1948.

—— "Progress of Political Theory between the Declaration of Independence and the Meeting of the Philadelphia Convention," *American Historical Review,* April, 1925, XXX, 511.

Dumbauld, Edward, *The Declaration of Independence and What It Means Today.* Norman, 1950.

Friedrich, C. J., *The Age of the Baroque,* New York, 1952.

Gabriel, Ralph H., *The Course of American Democratic Thought,* New York, 1940.

Gooch, G. P., *English Democratic Ideas in the Seventeenth Century,* Cambridge, 1927.

Hofstadter, Richard, *The American Political Tradition,* New York, 1949.

Holcombe, Arthur N., *Our More Perfect Union,* Cambridge, 1950.

Laski, Harold J., *Political Thought in England from Locke to Bentham,* London, 1920.

McIlwain, C. H., *The American Revolution,* New York, 1923.

Malone, Dumas, *Jefferson the Virginian,* Boston, 1948.

Miller, John C., *Origins of the American Revolution,* Boston, 1943.

Miller, Perry and Johnson, Thomas H., *The Puritans*, New York, 1938.

Nevins, Allen, *The American States During and After the Revolution*, New York, 1924.

Oliver, Frederick S., *Alexander Hamilton, an Essay on American Union*, New York, 1906.

Parrington, Vernon L., *Main Currents in American Thought.* 3 vols. New York, 1927.

Rossiter, Clinton L., *The Political Thought of the American Revolution*, New York, 1953.

Sabine, George H., *A History of Political Theory*, New York, 1937; revised ed. 1950.

Smith, J. Allen, *The Spirit of American Government*, New York, 1912.

Swisher, Carl B., *American Constitutional Development*, Boston, 1943.

Van Doren, Carl, *The Great Rehearsal*, New York, 1948.

Wertenbaker, T. J., *The Puritan Oligarchy*, New York, 1947.

Wilson, Francis G., *The American Political Mind*, New York, 1949.

Wormuth, Francis D., *The Origins of Modern Constitutionalism*, New York, 1948.

Wright, Benjamin F., *The Growth of American Constitutional Law*, Boston, 1942.

—— "The Origin of the Separation of Powers in America," *Economica*, XIII (May, 1931), p. 184.

THE BASIC DOCUMENTS

I

THE FOUNDATION OF THE UNION

THE DECLARATION OF INDEPENDENCE

[July 4, 1776]

The unanimous Declaration of the thirteen united States of America

WHEN IN THE COURSE OF HUMAN EVENTS, it becomes necessary for one people to dissolve the political bands which have connected them with another, and to assume among the Powers of the earth, the separate and equal station to which the Laws of Nature and of Nature's God entitle them, a decent respect to the opinions of mankind requires that they should declare the causes which impel them to the separation.

We hold these truths to be self-evident, that all men are created equal, that they are endowed by their Creator with certain unalienable Rights, that among these are Life, Liberty, and the pursuit of Happiness. That to secure these rights, Governments are instituted among Men, deriving their just powers from the consent of the governed; That whenever any Form of Government becomes destructive of these ends, it is the Right of the People to alter or to abolish it, and to institute new Government, laying its foundation on such principles and organizing its powers in such form, as to them shall seem most likely to effect their Safety and Happiness. Prudence, indeed, will dictate that Governments long established should not be changed for light and transient causes; and accordingly all experience hath shown, that mankind are more disposed to suffer, while evils are sufferable, than to right themselves by abolishing the forms to which they are accustomed. But when a long train of abuses and usurpations, pursuing invariably the same Object evinces a design to reduce them under absolute Despotism, it is their right, it is their duty, to throw off such Government, and to provide new Guards for their future security.—Such has been the patient sufferance of these Colonies;

and such is now the necessity which constrains them to alter their former Systems of Government. The history of the present King of Great Britain is a history of repeated injuries and usurpations, all having in direct object the establishment of an absolute Tyranny over these States. To prove this, let Facts be submitted to a candid world.

He has refused his Assent to Laws, the most wholesome and necessary for the public good.

He has forbidden his Governors to pass Laws of immediate and pressing importance, unless suspended in their operation till his Assent should be obtained; and when so suspended, he has utterly neglected to attend to them.

He has refused to pass other Laws for the accommodation of large districts of people, unless those people would relinquish the right of Representation in the Legislature, a right inestimable to them and formidable to tyrants only.

He has called together legislative bodies at places unusual, uncomfortable, and distant from the depository of their Public Records, for the sole purpose of fatiguing them into compliance with his measures.

He has dissolved Representative Houses repeatedly, for opposing with manly firmness his invasions on the rights of the people.

He has refused for a long time, after such dissolutions, to cause others to be elected; whereby the Legislative Powers, incapable of Annihilation, have returned to the People at large for their exercise; the State remaining in the meantime exposed to all the dangers of invasion from without, and convulsions within.

He has endeavoured to prevent the population of these States; for that purpose obstructing the Laws of Naturalization of Foreigners; refusing to pass others to encourage their migration hither, and raising the conditions of new Appropriations of Lands.

He has obstructed the Administration of Justice, by refusing his Assent to Laws for establishing Judiciary Powers.

He has made Judges dependent on his Will alone, for the

tenure of their offices, and the amount and payment of their salaries.

He has erected a multitude of New Offices, and sent hither swarms of Officers to harass our People, and eat out their substance.

He has kept among us, in times of peace, Standing Armies without the Consent of our legislature.

He has affected to render the Military independent of and superior to the Civil Power.

He has combined with others to subject us to a jurisdiction foreign to our constitution, and unacknowledged by our laws; giving his Assent to their acts of pretended legislation:

For quartering large bodies of armed troops among us:

For protecting them, by a mock Trial, from Punishment for any Murders which they should commit on the Inhabitants of these States:

For cutting off our Trade with all parts of the world:

For imposing taxes on us without our Consent:

For depriving us in many cases, of the benefits of Trial by Jury:

For transporting us beyond Seas to be tried for pretended offences:

For abolishing the free System of English Laws in a neighbouring Province, establishing therein an Arbitrary government, and enlarging its Boundaries so as to render it at once an example and fit instrument for introducing the same absolute rule into these Colonies:

For taking away our Charters, abolishing our most valuable Laws, and altering fundamentally the Forms of our Governments:

For suspending our own Legislature, and declaring themselves invested with Power to legislate for us in all cases whatsoever.

He has abdicated Government here, by declaring us out of his Protection and waging War against us.

He has plundered our seas, ravaged our Coasts, burnt our towns, and destroyed the lives of our people.

He is at this time transporting large armies of foreign mercenaries to compleat the works of death, desolation and tyranny, already begun with circumstances of Cruelty & perfidy scarcely paralleled in the most barbarous ages, and totally unworthy the Head of a civilized nation.

He has constrained our fellow Citizens taken Captive on the high Seas to bear Arms against their Country, to become the executioners of their friends and Brethren, or to fall themselves by their Hands.

He has excited domestic insurrections amongst us, and has endeavoured to bring on the inhabitants of our frontiers, the merciless Indian Savages, whose known rule of warfare, is an undistinguished destruction of all ages, sexes and conditions.

In every stage of these Oppressions We have Petitioned for Redress in the most humble terms: Our repeated Petitions have been answered only by repeated injury. A Prince, whose character is thus marked by every act which may define a Tyrant, is unfit to be the ruler of a free People.

Nor have We been wanting in attention to our British brethren. We have warned them from time to time of attempts by their legislature to extend an unwarrantable jurisdiction over us. We have reminded them of the circumstances of our emigration and settlement here. We have appealed to their native justice and magnanimity, and we have conjured them by the ties of our common kindred to disavow these usurpations, which would inevitably interrupt our connections and correspondence. They too have been deaf to the voice of justice and of consanguinity. We must, therefore, acquiesce in the necessity, which denounces our Separation, and hold them, as we hold the rest of mankind, Enemies in War, in Peace Friends.

We, therefore, the Representatives of the united States of America, in General Congress, Assembled, appealing to the Supreme Judge of the world for the rectitude of our intentions, do, in the Name, and by Authority of the good People of these Colonies, solemnly publish and declare, That these United Colonies are, and of Right ought to be Free and Independent States; that they are Absolved from all Allegiance to the British Crown, and that all political connection between them and the State of Great Britain, is and ought to be totally dissolved; and that as Free and Independent States, they have full Power to levy War, conclude Peace, contract Alliances, establish Commerce, and to do all other Acts and Things which Independent States may of right do. And for the support of this Declaration, with a firm reliance on the Protection of Divine Providence, we mutually pledge to each other our Lives, our Fortunes and our sacred Honor.

JOHN HANCOCK.

New Hampshire

JOSIAH BARTLETT
WM. WHIPPLE

MATTHEW THORNTON

Massachusetts Bay

SAML. ADAMS
JOHN ADAMS

ELBRIDGE GERRY
ROBT. TREAT PAINE

Rhode Island

STEP. HOPKINS

WILLIAM ELLERY

Connecticut

ROGER SHERMAN
SAM'EL HUNTINGTON

WM. WILLIAMS
OLIVER WOLCOTT

New York

WM. FLOYD
PHIL. LIVINGSTON

FRANS. LEWIS
LEWIS MORRIS

New Jersey

RICHD. STOCKTON
JNO. WITHERSPOON
FRAS. HOPKINSON

JOHN HART
ABRA. CLARK

Pennsylvania

ROBT. MORRIS
BENJAMIN RUSH
BENJA. FRANKLIN
JOHN MORTON
GEO. CLYMER

JAS. SMITH
GEO. TAYLOR
JAMES WILSON
GEO. ROSS

Delaware

CÆSAR RODNEY
GEO. READ

THO. M'KEAN

Maryland

SAMUEL CHASE
WM. PACA

THOS. STONE
CHARLES CARROLL of Carrollton

Virginia

GEORGE WYTHE
RICHARD HENRY LEE
TH. JEFFERSON
BENJA. HARRISON

THOS. NELSON, jr.
FRANCIS LIGHTFOOT LEE
CARTER BRAXTON

North Carolina

WM. HOOPER
JOSEPH HEWES

JOHN PENN

South Carolina

EDWARD RUTLEDGE
THOS. HEYWARD, junr.

ARTHUR MIDDLETON
THOMAS LYNCH, junr.

Georgia

BUTTON GWINNETT
LYMAN HALL

GEO. WALTON

ARTICLES OF CONFEDERATION

[*November 15, 1777*]

To all to whom these Presents shall come, we the undersigned Delegates of the States affixed to our Names send greeting.

WHEREAS THE DELEGATES of the United States of America in Congress assembled did on the fifteenth day of November in the year of our Lord One Thousand Seven Hundred and Seventy-seven, and in the Second Year of the Independence of America agree to certain articles of Confederation and perpetual Union between the States of Newhampshire, Massachusetts-bay, Rhodeisland and Providence Plantations, Connecticut, New York, New Jersey, Pennsylvania, Delaware, Virginia, North-Carolina, South-Carolina and Georgia in the Words following, viz.

"ARTICLES OF CONFEDERATION AND PERPETUAL UNION BETWEEN THE STATES OF NEWHAMPSHIRE, MASSACHUSETTS-BAY, RHODEISLAND AND PROVIDENCE PLANTATIONS, CONNECTICUT, NEW-YORK, NEW-JERSEY, PENNSYLVANIA, DELAWARE, MARYLAND, VIRGINIA, NORTH-CAROLINA, SOUTH-CAROLINA AND GEORGIA."

ARTICLE I. The stile of this confederacy shall be "The United States of America."

ARTICLE II. Each State retains its sovereignty, freedom and independence, and every power, jurisdiction and right, which is not by this confederation expressly delegated to the United States, in Congress assembled.

ARTICLE III. The said States hereby severally enter into a firm league of friendship with each other, for their common defence, the security of their liberties, and their mutual and general welfare, binding themselves to assist each other, against all force offered to, or attacks made upon them, or

9

any of them, on account of religion, sovereignty, trade, or any other pretence whatever.

ARTICLE IV. The better to secure and perpetuate mutual friendship and intercourse among the people of the different States in this Union, the free inhabitants of each of these States, paupers, vagabonds and fugitives from justice excepted, shall be entitled to all privileges and immunities of free citizens in the several States; and the people of each State shall have free ingress and regress to and from any other State, and shall enjoy therein all the privileges of trade and commerce, subject to the same duties, impositions and restrictions as the inhabitants thereof respectively, provided that such restrictions shall not extend so far as to prevent the removal of property imported into any State, to any other State of which the owner is an inhabitant; provided also that no imposition, duties or restriction shall be laid by any State, on the property of the United States, or either of them.

If any Person guilty of, or charged with treason, felony, or other high misdemeanor in any State, shall flee from justice, and be found in any of the United States, he shall upon demand of the Governor or Executive power, of the State from which he fled, be delivered up and removed to the State having jurisdiction of his offence.

Full faith and credit shall be given in each of these States to the records, acts and judicial proceedings of the courts and magistrates of every other State.

ARTICLE V. For the more convenient management of the general interest of the United States, delegates shall be annually appointed in such manner as the legislature of each State shall direct, to meet in Congress on the first Monday in November, in every year, with a power reserved to each State, to recall its delegates, or any of them, at any time within the year, and to send others in their stead, for the remainder of the year.

No State shall be represented in Congress by less than two, nor by more than seven members; and no person shall be capable of being a delegate for more than three years in any term of six years; nor shall any person, being a delegate, be capable of holding any office under the United States, for which he, or another for his benefit receives any salary, fees or emolument of any kind.

Each State shall maintain its own delegates in a meeting of the States, and while they act as members of the committee of the States.

In determining questions in the United States, in Congress assembled, each State shall have one vote.

Freedom of speech and debate in Congress shall not be impeached or questioned in any court, or place out of Congress, and the members of Congress shall be protected in their persons from arrests and imprisonments, during the time of their going to and from, and attendance on Congress, except for treason, felony, or breach of the peace.

ARTICLE VI. No State without the consent of the United States in Congress assembled, shall send any embassy to, or receive any embassy from, or enter into any conference, agreement, alliance or treaty with any king, prince or state; nor shall any person holding any office of profit or trust under the United States, or any of them, accept of any present, emolument, office or title of any kind whatever from any king, prince or foreign state; nor shall the United States in Congress assembled, or any of them, grant any title of nobility.

No two or more States shall enter into any treaty, confederation or alliance whatever between them, without the consent of the United States in Congress assembled, specifying accurately the purposes for which the same is to be entered into, and how long it shall continue.

No State shall lay any imposts or duties, which may interfere with any stipulations in treaties, entered into by the United States in Congress assembled, with any king, prince or state, in pursuance of any treaties already proposed by Congress, to the courts of France and Spain.

No vessels of war shall be kept up in time of peace by any

State, except such number only, as shall be deemed necessary by the United States in Congress assembled, for the defence of such State, or its trade; nor shall any body of forces be kept up by any State, in time of peace, except such number only, as in the judgment of the United States, in Congress assembled, shall be deemed requisite to garrison the forts necessary for the defence of such State; but every State shall always keep up a well regulated and disciplined militia, sufficiently armed and accoutered, and shall provide and constantly have ready for use, in public stores, a due number of field pieces and tents, and a proper quantity of arms, ammunition and camp equipage.

No State shall engage in any war without the consent of the United States in Congress assembled, unless such State be actually invaded by enemies, or shall have received certain advice of a resolution being formed by some nation of Indians to invade such State, and the danger is so imminent as not to admit of a delay, till the United States in Congress assembled can be consulted: nor shall any State grant commissions to any ships or vessels of war, nor letters of marque or reprisal, except it be after a declaration of war by the United States in Congress assembled, and then only against the kingdom or state and the subjects thereof, against which war has been so declared, and under such regulations as shall be established by the United States in Congress assembled, unless such State be infested by pirates, in which case vessels of war may be fitted out for that occasion, and kept so long as the danger shall continue, or until the United States in Congress assembled shall determine otherwise.

ARTICLE VII.   When land-forces are raised by any State for the common defence, all officers of or under the rank of colonel, shall be appointed by the Legislature of each State respectively by whom such forces shall be raised, or in such manner as such State shall direct, and all vacancies shall be filled up by the State which first made the appointment.

ARTICLE VIII.   All charges of war, and all other expenses

that shall be incurred for the common defence or general welfare, and allowed by the United States in Congress assembled, shall be defrayed out of a common treasury, which shall be supplied by the several States, in proportion to the value of all land within each State, granted to or surveyed for any person, as such land and the buildings and improvements thereon shall be estimated according to such mode as the United States in Congress assembled, shall from time to time direct and appoint.

The taxes for paying that proportion shall be laid and levied by the authority and direction of the Legislatures of the several States within the time agreed upon by the United States in Congress assembled.

ARTICLE IX. The United States in Congress assembled, shall have the sole and exclusive right and power of determining on peace and war, except in the cases mentioned in the sixth article—of sending and receiving ambassadors—entering into treaties and alliances, provided that no treaty of commerce shall be made whereby the legislative power of the respective States shall be restrained from imposing such imposts and duties on foreigners, as their own people are subjected to, or from prohibiting the exportation or importation of any species of goods or commodities whatsoever—of establishing rules for deciding in all cases, what captures on land or water shall be legal, and in what manner prizes taken by land or naval forces in the service of the United States shall be divided or appropriated—of granting letters of marque and reprisal in times of peace—appointing courts for the trial of piracies and felonies committed on the high seas and establishing courts for receiving and determining finally appeals in all cases of captures, provided that no member of Congress shall be appointed a judge of any of the said courts.

The United States in Congress assembled shall also be the last resort on appeal in all disputes and differences now subsisting or that hereafter may arise between two or more States concerning boundary, jurisdiction or any other cause whatever; which authority shall always be exercised in the manner following. Whenever the legislative or executive authority or lawful agent of any State in controversy with another shall present a petition to Congress, stating the matter in question and praying for a hearing, notice thereof shall be given by order of Congress to the legislative or executive authority of the other State in controversy, and a day assigned for the appearance of the parties by their lawful agents, who shall then be directed to appoint by joint consent, commissioners or judges to constitute a court for hearing and determining the matter in question: but if they cannot agree, Congress shall name three persons out of each of the United States, and from the list of such persons each party shall alternately strike out one, the petitioners beginning, until the number shall be reduced to thirteen; and from that number not less than seven, or more than nine names as Congress shall direct, shall in the presence of Congress be drawn out by lot, and the persons whose names shall be so drawn or any five of them, shall be commissioners or judges, to hear and finally determine the controversy, so always as a major part of the judges who shall hear the cause shall agree in the determination: and if either party shall neglect to attend at the day appointed, without showing reasons, which Congress shall judge sufficient, or being present shall refuse to strike, the Congress shall proceed to nominate three persons out of each State, and the Secretary of Congress shall strike in behalf of such party absent or re-fusing; and the judgment and sentence of the court to be appointed, in the manner before prescribed, shall be final and conclusive; and if any of the parties shall refuse to submit to the authority of such court, or to appear or defend their claim or cause, the court shall nevertheless proceed to pronounce sentence, or judgment, which shall in like manner be final and decisive, the judgment or sentence and other proceed-ings being in either case transmitted to Congress, and lodged among the acts of Congress for the security of the parties con-cerned: provided that every commissioner, before he sits in judgment, shall take an oath to be administered by one of the judges of the supreme or superior court of the State, where the cause shall be tried, "well and truly to hear and determine the matter in question, according to the best of his judgment, without favour, affection or hope of reward:" provided also that no State shall be deprived of territory for the benefit of the United States.

All controversies concerning the private right of soil claimed under different grants of two or more States, whose jurisdiction as they may respect such lands, and the States which passed such grants are adjusted, the said grants or either of them being at the same time claimed to have originated antecedent to such settlement of jurisdiction, shall on the petition of either party to the Congress of the United States, be finally determined as near as may be in the same manner as is before prescribed for deciding disputes respecting territorial jurisdiction between different States.

The United States in Congress assembled shall also have the sole and exclusive right and power of regulating the alloy and value of coin struck by their own authority, or by that of the respective States—fixing the standard of weights and measures throughout the United States—regulating the trade and managing all affairs with the Indians, not members of any of the States, provided that the legislative right of any State within its own limits be not infringed or violated—establishing and regulating post-offices from one State to another, throughout all the United States, and exacting such postage on the papers passing thro' the same as may be requisite to defray the expenses of the said office—appointing all officers of the land forces, in the service of the United States, excepting regimental officers—appointing all the officers of the naval forces, and commissioning all officers whatever in the service of the United States—making rules for the government and regulation of the said land and naval forces, and directing their operations.

The United States in Congress assembled shall have authority to appoint a committee, to sit in the recess of Congress, to be denominated "a Committee of the States," and to consist of one delegate from each State; and to appoint such other committees and civil officers as may be necessary for managing the general affairs of the United States under their direction —to appoint one of their number to preside, provided that no person be allowed to serve in the office of president more than one year in any term of three years; to ascertain the necessary sums of money to be raised for the service of the United States, and to appropriate and apply the same for defraying the public expenses—to borrow money, or emit bills on the credit of the United States, transmitting every half year to the respective States an account of the sums of money so borrowed or emitted,—to build and equip a navy—to agree upon the number of land forces, and to make requisitions from each State for its quota, in proportion to the number of white inhabitants in such State; which requisition shall be binding, and thereupon the Legislature of each State shall appoint the regimental officers, raise the men and cloath, arm and equip them in a soldier like manner, at the expense of the United States; and the officers and men so cloathed, armed and equipped shall march to the place appointed, and within the time agreed on by the United States in Congress assembled: but if the United States in Congress assembled shall, on consideration of circumstances judge proper that any State should not raise men, or should raise a smaller number than its quota, and that any other State should raise a greater number of men than the quota thereof, such extra number shall be raised, officered, cloathed, armed and equipped in the same as the quota of such State, unless the Legislature of such State shall judge that such extra number cannot be safely spared outside of the same, in which case they shall raise, officer, cloath, arm and equip as many of such extra number as they judge can be safely spared. And the officers and men so cloathed, armed and equipped, shall march to the place appointed, and within the time agreed on by the United States in Congress assembled.

The United States in Congress assembled shall never engage in a war, nor grant letters of marque and reprisal in time of peace, nor enter into any treaties or alliances, nor coin money, nor regulate the value thereof, nor ascertain the sums and expenses necessary for the defence and welfare of the United States, or any of them, nor emit bills, nor borrow money on the credit of the United States, nor appropriate money, nor agree upon the number of vessels of war, to be built or purchased, or the number of land or sea forces to be raised, nor appoint a commander in chief of the army or navy, unless nine States assent to the same: nor shall a question on any other point, except for adjourning from day to day be determined, unless by the votes of a majority of the United States in Congress assembled.

The Congress of the United States shall have power to adjourn to any time within the year, and to any place within the United States, so that no period of adjournment be for a longer duration than the space of six months, and shall publish the journal of their proceedings monthly, except such parts thereof relating to treaties, alliances or military operations, as in their judgment require secrecy; and the yeas and nays of the delegates of each State on any question shall be entered on the journal, when it is desired by any delegate; and the delegates of a State, or any of them, at his or their request shall be furnished with a transcript of the said journal, except such parts as are above excepted, to lay before the Legislatures of the several States.

ARTICLE X. The committee of the States, or any nine of them, shall be authorized to execute, in the recess of Congress, such of the powers of Congress as the United States in Congress assembled, by the consent of nine States, shall from time to time think expedient to vest them with; provided that no power be delegated to the said committee, for the exercise of which, by the articles of confederation, the voice of nine States in the Congress of the United States assembled is requisite.

ARTICLE XI. Canada acceding to this confederation, and joining in the measures of the United States, shall be admitted into, and entitled to all the advantages of this Union: but no other colony shall be admitted into the same, unless such admission be agreed to by nine States.

ARTICLE XII. All bills of credit emitted, monies borrowed and debts contracted by, or under the authority of Congress, before the assembling of the United States, in pursuance of the present confederation, shall be deemed and considered as a charge against the United States, for payment and satisfaction whereof the said United States, and the public faith are hereby solemnly pledged.

ARTICLE XIII. Every State shall abide by the determinations of the United States in Congress assembled, on all questions which by this confederation are submitted to them. And the articles of this confederation shall be inviolably observed by every State, and the Union shall be perpetual; nor shall any alteration at any time hereafter be made in any of them; unless such alteration be agreed to in a Congress of the United States, and be afterwards confirmed by the Legislatures of every State.

And WHEREAS it hath pleased the Great Governor of the World to incline the hearts of the Legislatures we respectively represent in Congress, to approve of, and to authorize us to ratify the said articles of confederation and perpetual union. Know ye that we the undersigned delegates, by virtue of the power and authority to us given for that purpose, do by these presents, in the name and in behalf of our respective constituents, fully and entirely ratify and confirm each and every of the said articles of confederation and perpetual union, and all and singular the matters and things therein contained: and we do further solemnly plight and engage the faith of our respective constituents, that they shall abide by the determinations of the United States in Congress assembled, on all questions, which by the said confederation are submitted to them. And that the articles thereof shall be inviolably observed by the States we respectively represent, and that the Union shall be perpetual.

In witness whereof we have hereunto set our hands in Congress. Done at Philadelphia in the State of Pennsylvania the ninth day of July in the year of our Lord one thousand seven hundred and seventy-eight, and in the third year of the independence of America.

On the part & behalf of the State of New Hampshire

JOSIAH BARTLETT   JOHN WENTWORTH, Junr
                                    August 8th, 1778

On the part and behalf of the State of Massachusetts Bay

JOHN HANCOCK   FRANCIS DANA
SAMUEL ADAMS   JAMES LOVELL
ELBRIDGE GERRY   SAMUEL HOLTEN

On the part and behalf of the State of Rhode Island and Providence Plantations

WILLIAM ELLERY   JOHN COLLINS
HENRY MARCHANT

On the part and behalf of the State of Connecticut

ROGER SHERMAN   TITUS HOSMER
SAMUEL HUNTINGTON   ANDREW ADAMS
OLIVER WOLCOTT

On the part and behalf of the State of New York

JAS. DUANE   GOUV. MORRIS
FRA. LEWIS   WM. DUER

On the part and in behalf of the State of New Jersey Novr. 26, 1778

JNO. WITHERSPOON   NATHL. SCUDDER

On the part and behalf of the State of Pennsylvania

ROBT. MORRIS   WILLIAM CLINGAN
DANIEL ROBERDEAU   JOSEPH REED, 22d July,
JNO. BAYARD SMITH   1778

On the part & behalf of the State of Delaware

THOS. M'KEAN, Feby. 12,   JOHN DICKINSON, May 5th,
   1779   1779
NICHOLAS VAN DYKE

On the part and behalf of the State of Maryland

JOHN HANSON, March 1,   DANIEL CARROLL, Mar. 1,
   1781   1781

On the part and behalf of the State of Virginia

RICHARD HENRY LEE   JNO. HARVIE
JOHN BANISTER   FRANCIS LIGHTFOOT LEE
THOMAS ADAMS

On the part and behalf of the State of No. Carolina

JOHN PENN, July 21, 1778   JNO. WILLIAMS
CORNS. HARNETT

On the part & behalf of the State of South Carolina

HENRY LAURENS   RICHD. HUTSON
WILLIAM HENRY DRAYTON   THOS. HEYWARD, Junr
JNO. MATTHEWS

On the part & behalf of the State of Georgia

EDWD. TELFAIR   EDWD. LANGWORTHY
JNO. WALTON, 24th July,
   1778

THE BASIC DOCUMENTS

II
THE CONSTITUTION IN THE MAKING

RESOLUTION OF CONGRESS

[*February 21, 1787*]

WHEREAS THERE IS PROVISION in the Articles of Confederation & perpetual Union for making alterations therein by the Assent of a Congress of the United States and of the legislatures of the several States; And whereas experience hath evinced that there are defects in the present Confederation, as a means to remedy which several of the States and particularly the State of New York by express instruction to their delegates in Congress have suggested a convention for the purposes expressed in the following resolution and such Convention appearing to be the most probable means of establishing in these states a firm national government.

Resolved that in the opinion of Congress it is expedient that on the second Monday in May next a Convention of delegates who shall have been appointed by the several states be held at Philadelphia for the sole and express purpose of revising the Articles of Confederation and reporting to Congress and the several legislatures such alterations and provisions therein as shall when agreed to in Congress and confirmed by the states render the federal constitution adequate to the exigencies of Government & the preservation of the Union.

THE VIRGINIA PLAN AS OFFERED BY RANDOLPH

[*May 29, 1787*]

1. RESOLVED, That the articles of Confederation ought to be so corrected and enlarged as to accomplish the objects proposed by their institution; namely, common defence, security of liberty and general welfare.

2. RESOLVED, therefore, That the rights of suffrage, in the National Legislature ought to be proportioned to the Quotas of contribution, or to the number of free inhabitants, as the one or the other rule may seem best in different cases.

3. RESOLVED, That the National Legislature ought to consist of two branches.

4. RESOLVED, That the members of the first branch of the National Legislature ought to be elected by the people of the several States every   for the term of   ; to be of the age of   years at least; to receive liberal stipends by which they may be compensated for the devotion of their time to public service; to be ineligible to any office established by a particular State, or under the authority of the United States, except those peculiarly belonging to the functions of the first branch, during the term of service, and for the space of after its expiration; to be incapable of re-election for the space of   after the expiration of their term of service; and to be subject to recall.

5. RESOLVED, That the members of the second branch of the National Legislature ought to be elected by those of the first, out of a proper number of persons nominated by the individual Legislatures; to be of the age of   years, at least; to hold their offices for a term sufficient to ensure their independency; to receive liberal stipends, by which they may be compensated for the devotion of their time to public service; and to be ineligible to any office established by a particular State, or under the authority of the United States, except those pe-

culiarly belonging to the functions of the second branch, during the term of service, and for the space of   after the expiration thereof.

6. RESOLVED, That each branch ought to possess the right of originating Acts; that the National Legislature ought to be impowered to enjoy the Legislative Rights vested in Congress by the Confederation, and moreover to legislate in all cases to which the separate States are incompetent, or in which the harmony of the United States may be interrupted by the exercise of individual Legislation; to negative all laws passed by the several States, contravening in the opinion of the National Legislature the articles of Union; and to call forth the force of the Union against any member of the Union failing to fulfil its duty under the articles thereof.

7. RESOLVED, That a national executive be instituted; to be chosen by the National Legislature for the term of   years; to receive punctually at stated times, a fixed compensation for the services rendered, in which no increase or diminution shall be made so as to affect the Magistracy existing at the time of increase or diminution; and to be ineligible a second time; and that besides a general authority to execute the National laws, it ought to enjoy the Executive rights vested in Congress by the Confederation.

8. RESOLVED, That the executive and a convenient number of the National Judiciary, ought to compose a council of revision with authority to examine every act of the National Legislature before it shall operate, and every act of a particular Legislature before a Negative thereon shall be final; and that the dissent of the said Council shall amount to a rejection, unless the act of the National Legislature be again passed, or that of a particular Legislature be again negatived by   of the members of each branch.

9. RESOLVED, That a national judiciary be established to consist of one or more supreme tribunals, and of inferior tribunals to be chosen by the National Legislature, to hold their offices during good behaviour; and to receive punctually at stated times fixed compensations for their services, in which no in-

crease or diminution shall be made so as to affect the person actually in office at the time of such increase or diminution. That the jurisdiction of the inferior tribunals shall be to hear and determine in the first instance, and of the supreme tribunal to hear and determine, in the dernier resort, all piracies and felonies on the high seas; captures from an enemy; cases in which foreigners or citizens of other States applying to such jurisdictions may be interested, or which respect the collection of the National revenue; impeachments of any National officer; and questions which involve the national peace or harmony.

10. RESOLVED, That provision ought to be made for the admission of States lawfully arising within the limits of the United States, whether from a voluntary junction of Government and Territory, or otherwise, with the consent of a number of voices in the National Legislature less than the whole.

11. RESOLVED, That a Republican Government and the territory of each State, except in the instance of a voluntary junction of Government and territory, ought to be guaranteed by the United States to each State.

12. RESOLVED, That provision ought to be made for the continuance of Congress and their authorities and privileges, until a given day after the reform of the articles of Union shall be adopted, and for the completion of all their engagements.

13. RESOLVED, That provision ought to be made for the amendment of the articles of Union whensoever it shall seem necessary; and that the assent of the National Legislature ought not to be required thereto.

14. RESOLVED, That the legislative, executive, and judiciary powers within the several States, ought to be bound by oath to support the articles of union.

15. RESOLVED, That the amendments which shall be offered to the Confederation, by the Convention ought at a proper time, or times, after the approbation of Congress, to be submitted to an assembly or assemblies of Representatives, recommended by the several Legislatures to be expressly chosen by the people, to consider and decide thereon.

THE VIRGINIA PLAN AS REPORTED BY THE COMMITTEE OF THE WHOLE [1]

[*June 13, 1787*]

1. RESOLVED, That it is the opinion of this Committee, that a national government ought to be established, consisting of a Supreme Legislative, Judiciary, and Executive.

2. RESOLVED, That the National Legislature ought to consist of Two Branches.

3. RESOLVED, That the Members of the first branch of the national Legislature ought to be elected by the People of the several States, for the term of Three years; to receive fixed stipends, by which they may be compensated for the devotion of their time to public service, to be paid out of the National Treasury; to be ineligible to any Office established by a particular State, or under the authority of the United States (except those peculiarly belonging to the functions of the first branch) during the term of service, and under the national government for the space of one year after its expiration.

4. RESOLVED, That the Members of the second Branch of the national Legislature ought to be chosen by the individual Legislatures; to be of the age of thirty years at least; to hold their offices for a term sufficient to ensure their independency, namely, seven years; to receive fixed stipends, by which they may be compensated for the devotion of their time to public service, to be paid out of the National Treasury; to be ineligible to any Office established by a particular State, or under the authority of the United States (except those peculiarly belonging to the functions of the second branch) during the term of service, and under the national government, for the space of one Year after its expiration.

5. RESOLVED, That each branch ought to possess the right of originating acts.

1 The text follows Farrand's *Records of the Federal Convention* I, 228-32, as rearranged by Carl Van Doren in his *The Great Rehearsal* (1948), used by permission of the publishers, The Viking Press.

6. RESOLVED, That the national Legislature ought to be empowered to enjoy the legislative rights vested in Congress by the confederation; and moreover to legislate in all cases to which the separate States are incompetent, or in which the harmony of the United States may be interrupted by the exercise of individual legislation; to negative all laws passed by the several States contravening, in the opinion of the national legislature, the articles of union, or any treaties subsisting under the authority of the union.

7. RESOLVED, That the right of suffrage in the first branch of the national Legislature ought not to be according to the rule established in the articles of confederation, but according to some equitable ratio of representation; namely, in proportion to the whole number of white and other free citizens and inhabitants, of every age, sex, and condition, including those bound to servitude for a term of years, and three fifths of all other persons not comprehended in the foregoing description, except Indians not paying taxes in each State.

8. RESOLVED, That the right of suffrage in the second branch of the national Legislature ought to be according to the rule established for the first.

9. RESOLVED, That a national Executive be instituted to consist of a Single Person; to be chosen by the National Legislature, for the term of Seven years; with power to carry into execution the National Laws; to appoint to Offices in cases not otherwise provided for; to be ineligible the second time; and to be removable on impeachment and conviction of malpractice, or neglect of duty; to receive a fixed stipend, by which he may be compensated for the devotion of his time to public service, to be paid out of the national Treasury.

10. RESOLVED, That the national executive shall have a right to negative any legislative act, which shall not be afterwards passed unless by two third parts of each branch of the national Legislature.

11. RESOLVED, That a national Judiciary be established to consist of One supreme Tribunal; the Judges of which to be appointed by the second Branch of the National Legislature;

to hold their offices during good behaviour; to receive punctually, at stated times, a fixed compensation for their services, in which no increase or diminution shall be made, so as to affect the persons actually in office at the time of such increase or diminution.

12. RESOLVED, That the national Legislature be empowered to appoint inferior Tribunals.

13. RESOLVED, That the jurisdiction of the national Judiciary shall extend to cases which respect the collection of the national revenue; impeachments of any National officers; and questions which involve the national peace and harmony.

14. RESOLVED, That provision ought to be made for the admission of States, lawfully arising within the limits of the United States, whether from a voluntary junction of government and territory, or otherwise, with the consent of a number of voices in the National legislature less than the whole.

15. RESOLVED, That provision ought to be made for the continuance of Congress and their authorities until a given day after the reform of the articles of Union shall be adopted; and for the completion of all their engagements.

16. RESOLVED, That a republican Constitution, and its existing laws, ought to be guaranteed to each State by the United States.

17. RESOLVED, That provision ought to be made for the amendment of the articles of Union, whensoever it shall seem necessary.

18. RESOLVED, That the Legislative, Executive, and Judiciary powers within the several States ought to be bound by oath to support the articles of Union.

19. RESOLVED, That the amendments which shall be offered to the confederation by the Convention, ought at a proper time or times, after the approbation of Congress, to be submitted to an assembly or assemblies of representatives, recommended by the several Legislatures, to be submitted to an assembly or assemblies of representatives, recommended by the several Legislatures, to be expressly chosen by the People to consider and decide thereon.

THE NEW JERSEY PLAN AS OFFERED BY PATERSON

[*June 15, 1787*]

1. RESOLVED, That the articles of Confederation ought to be so revised, corrected and enlarged, as to render the federal Constitution adequate to the exigencies of Government, and the preservation of the Union.

2. RESOLVED, That in addition to the powers vested in the United States in Congress, by the present existing articles of Confederation, they be authorized to pass acts for raising a revenue, by levying a duty or duties on all goods and merchandizes of foreign growth or manufacture, imported into any part of the United States, by Stamps on paper, vellum, or parchment, and by a postage on all letters and packages passing through the general post-office, to be applied to such federal purposes as they shall deem proper and expedient; to make rules and regulations for the collection thereof; and the same from time to time, to alter and amend in such manner as they shall think proper; to pass Acts for the regulation of trade and commerce, as well with foreign nations as with each other: provided that all punishments, fines, forfeitures, and penalties to be incurred for contravening such rules and regulations shall be adjudged by the Common law Judiciarys of the State in which any offence contrary to the true intent and meaning of such Acts, rules and regulations shall have been committed or perpetrated, with liberty of commencing in the first instance all suits or prosecutions for that purpose, in the superior Common law Judiciary of such State; subject nevertheless, for the correction of all errors, both in law and fact in rendering judgment, to an appeal to the Judiciary of the United States.

3. RESOLVED, That whenever requisitions shall be necessary, instead of the rule for making requisitions mentioned in the articles of Confederation the United States in Congress be

authorized to make such requisitions in proportion to the whole number of white and other free citizens and inhabitants of every age, sex, and condition, including those bound to servitude for a term of years, and three fifths of all other persons not comprehended in the foregoing description, except Indians not paying taxes; that if such requisitions be not complied with, in the time specified therein, to direct the collection thereof in the non-complying States, and for that purpose to devise and pass acts directing and authorizing the same; provided that none of the powers hereby vested in the United States in Congress shall be exercised without the consent of at least   States; and in that proportion, if the number of confederated States should hereafter be increased or diminished.

4. RESOLVED, That the United States in Congress be authorized to elect a federal Executive to consist of   persons, to continue in office for the term of   years; to receive punctually at stated times a fixed compensation for their services in which no increase or diminution shall be made so as to affect the persons composing the Executive at the time of such increase or diminution, to be paid out of the federal treasury; to be incapable of holding any other office or appointment during their term of service, and for   years thereafter; to be ineligible a second time, and removable by Congress on application by a majority of the Executives of the several States. That the executive, besides their general authority to execute the federal acts ought to appoint all federal officers not otherwise provided for, and to direct all military operations; provided, that none of the persons composing the federal executive shall on any occasion take command of any troops, so as personally to conduct any military enterprise as General, or in any other capacity.

5. RESOLVED, That a federal Judiciary be established, to consist of a supreme Tribunal the Judges of which to be appointed by the Executive, and to hold their offices during good behaviour; to receive punctually at stated times a fixed compensation for their services, in which no increase or diminu-

tion shall be made, so as to affect the persons actually in office at the time of such increase or diminution. That the Judiciary so established shall have authority to hear and determine in the first instance on all impeachments of federal officers, and by way of appeal in the dernier resort in all cases touching the rights and privileges of Ambassadors; in all cases of captures from an enemy; in all cases of piracies and felonies on the high seas; in all cases in which foreigners may be interested, in the construction of any treaty or treaties, or which may arise on any of the acts for regulation of trade, or the collection of the federal Revenue. That none of the Judiciary shall during the time they remain in Office be capable of receiving or holding any other office or appointment during their term of service, or for   thereafter.

6. RESOLVED, That all acts of the United States in Congress, made by virtue and in pursuance of the powers hereby and by the articles of confederation vested in them, and all treaties made and ratified under the authority of the United States, shall be the supreme law of the respective States as far forth as those Acts or Treaties shall relate to the said States or their Citizens; and that the judiciary of the several States shall be bound thereby in their decisions, anything in the respective laws of the Individual States to the contrary notwithstanding; and if any State, or any body of men in any State, shall oppose or prevent the carrying into execution such acts or treaties, the federal Executive shall be authorized to call forth the powers of the Confederated States, or so much thereof as may be necessary, to enforce and compel an obedience to such Acts, or an Observance of such Treaties.

7. RESOLVED, That provision be made for the admission of new States into the Union.

8. RESOLVED, That the rule for naturalization ought to be the same in every State.

9. RESOLVED, That a citizen of one State committing an offence in another State of the Union shall be deemed guilty of the same offence as if it had been committed by a citizen of the State in which the offence was committed.

THE BASIC DOCUMENTS

III
THE CONSTITUTION

A BRIEF SUMMARY

Although most of the principal provisions of the Constitution have been touched on in the introductory essay, it may be useful at this point to set down a brief, systematic analysis of the document, to serve the purposes of both summary and clarification.

I. GENERAL PRINCIPLES OF THE CONSTITUTION

1. The nature of the Union. The American nation has been identified in a phrase quoted elsewhere in these pages as "an indestructible Union, composed of indestructible States," [1] and this "perpetual" character of the constitutional arrangement has been recognized both in law and fact since the Civil War, and in theory long before that. The textual warrants for this description are comparatively meager: for one, it has been argued that the Articles of Confederation were declared to be perpetual and that the Preamble to the Constitution declares that the object is "to form a more perfect Union"; hence the perpetuity of the present Union is inevitably implied. For another thing, it can be argued that, although the Constitution provides a method by which states are admitted to the Union (see Article IV, Section 3), it sets up no machinery for secession from it and recognizes no such possibility, unless the amending clause be so regarded (Article V). Presumably, the power of amendment might ratify a state's choice to leave the Union (although a theoretical dissent even to this might be made), but otherwise the constitutional text is said to imply an indissoluble arrangement. In any case, the words of the Constitution aside, the Civil War settled the question of indestructibility on a *de facto* basis, and surely nothing except war or the amending power can alter that status. As for the amending power itself, although it might be regarded as theoretically limited

[1] Texas v. White, 7 Wall. 700 (1869).

35

in some respects, the only recognized legal limitation is the denial, in Article V, of the power to alter the principle of equal representation in the Senate.

2. *The Separation of Powers.* The Constitution makes no specific reference to this principle, but it has always been assumed that the idea is implied by the opening sentences in Articles I, II, and III, i.e. "All legislative powers herein granted shall be vested in a Congress," etc. The use of the terms "legislative," "executive," and "judicial" respectively imports a division of governmental power between these three departments. The courts have, however, been lenient in permitting Congress to delegate its legislative power to the executive, and the line of distinction between the legislative and executive function is now somewhat blurred. Nevertheless, an attempt by the President to legislate *without* Congressional authorization, or a direct attempt by the Congress to assume an executive power, could still be invalidated on the basis of this principle.

3. *The Nation and the States.* The principal clauses of the Constitution relating to national-state relationships specifically are "the supremacy clause" of Article VI, Section 2, and the Tenth Amendment. The supremacy clause has been called "the linchpin of the Constitution," since it has the effect of binding the whole fabric of national government together. In practice, it means that a legitimately passed national law overrides a conflicting state law, even though the state act is otherwise valid; and that the legislation and judicial proceedings of the states are subject to review by the Supreme Court of the United States (see below). The Tenth Amendment declares the principle of "delegated" and "reserved" powers, i.e. that the national government can exercise only the powers enumerated in the Constitution and that all other proper functions of government are retained by the states. This idea was supposed to be implicit in the original Constitution, and the Tenth Amendment merely makes it explicit. In addition to these provisions, judicial construction alone has inhibited the states in certain ways as to their dealings with the Nation. For example, it has been held that some kinds

of state trade regulations are forbidden because they invade the "dormant" commerce power of Congress; and that the states may not directly tax an instrumentality of the federal government (a prohibition which has also been applied in reverse, so as to restrict the national government in taxing the states). Neither of these legal concepts is expressed in any specific clause of the Constitution; they are said to arise from the nature of the federal system itself.

4. Interstate Relations. The provisions in Article IV, Sections 1 and 2, relating to this subject are survivals of the interstate comity provisions of the Articles of Confederation. Other provisions are the "interstate compact" clause of Article I, Section 10, Paragraph 3, whose possibilities as a source of interstate cooperation are only recently being realized; and the arrangement in Article III, Section 2, which gives the federal judiciary jurisdiction over interstate disputes. Finally, the commerce clause has been held to prevent the states from erecting commercial barriers against their neighbors, so as to favor their own citizens at the expense of the rest of the nation.

5. Elections. The power to prescribe voting qualifications was left, in the original Constitution, to the several states, though with some qualifications; and subsequent amendments have extended these qualifications much further. Article I, Section 2, provides that those who vote for Representatives must have the qualifications of those who vote for the most numerous branch of the state legislature; and the Seventeenth Amendment prescribes the same qualifications for those who elect Senators. The states are also forbidden to deny the suffrage on the grounds of race or color (Amendment Fifteen) and on the ground of sex (Amendment Nineteen). The right to cast a vote for federal officers in accordance with valid state regulations can be protected by Congressional legislation. As for election to the presidency, the states are left free to prescribe qualifications to vote for the Electoral College (subject of course to Amendments Fifteen and Nineteen), and it was originally assumed that the Electors so chosen would make a free choice. But in practice the Electors

have followed the guidance of the voters, and the effect
is that the President is chosen by direct vote.

6. Citizenship. The Fourteenth Amendment grants
citizenship in both the nation and the state of residence to
all persons born in the United States (with certain minor
exceptions) and to all persons naturalized therein. Naturalization is achieved in accordance with Congressional law
passed under the authority of Article I, Section 8; and the
privilege of citizenship may be and is extended by Congress to persons born abroad of parents who are citizens.

II. THE POWERS OF THE NATION

1. The Powers of Congress. Most of the important
powers of Congress are grouped in Article I, Section 8,
although authorizations of various kinds are scattered
throughout the Constitution. The powers most often in-
voked to justify legislation have been, especially in recent
years, the commerce power and the "war power." The
authority to regulate interstate and foreign commerce is,
of course, specifically set forth in Section 8, but the general war power is inferred from various sources, including
paragraphs 11 to 14 of that Section. Under the authority
of these powers, as presently construed, the scope of federal
legislation is very broad. In fact it is difficult to imagine
just where their practical limits may lie, since no court
has prescribed them. The breadth of these, like the other
delegated powers, is immeasurably extended by the so-
called "elastic clause" of paragraph 18 which authorizes
Congress to pass any law which seems a convenient means
for carrying out the powers expressly delegated. Other
highly significant sources of congressional authority are the
tax power, once sharply restricted by judicial decision, but
now nearly unlimited; the power to control currency, derived chiefly from paragraph 5; and the power to tax
and spend for the general welfare, set forth in paragraph
1. Still other important powers in other sections of the
Constitution are the authority to prescribe the "times,
places, and manner" of holding elections for Congress
(Article I, Section 4); the investigatory power, whose

existence is inferred from the nature of the legislative function; and the power to control the appellate jurisdiction of the Supreme Court (Article III, Section 2). The upshot of this impressive array of authority—and the list could be extended substantially—is that the Congress is endowed with the full range of powers generally expected of a sovereign nation and that, constitutionally speaking, it stands forth as the dominant branch of the federal triumvirate.

2. *The Powers of the President.* The Constitution makes the President an extremely potent executive. Article I, Section 2, specifically makes him commander-in-chief of the nation's armed forces, grants him broad control over the foreign policy of the United States through the treaty-making power and authority over the administrative agencies of government through the power of appointment and removal. It is true that the Senate participates in both the treaty-making and appointment process, and that body is by no means negligible. But the President, in the nature of the case, holds the initiative, and this means that he is usually the dominant partner with respect to these functions. The distinguishing characteristic of the president's constitutional authority is, however, its vagueness. His authority as commander-in-chief and his duty to "take care that the laws be faithfully executed" (Article II, Section III) are both hard to define, and some commentators have made much of them. Moreover, it had been argued that the bestowal of "the executive power" vests him with general authority to perform the acts appropriate to that function, quite apart from any explicit constitutional or congressional mandate. At all events, it is clear that he is a very powerful figure. His position relative to the Congress probably depends, not so much upon the Constitution, as upon the facts of political life at any given time.

3. *The Judicial Power.* The salient facts about the judicial power are two: the authority to review the acts and judicial decisions of the states, which is supposedly derived from the "supremacy clause" and from the implications of Article III; and the authority to review acts of

the President and the Congress in the light of their constitutionality. The latter power has been tenuously attached to various provisions of the Constitution by judges bent on asserting it, but the fact is that the institution of judicial review over acts of Congress derives from no specific constitutional clause, but is inferred from the nature of the judicial function. It seems probable that the Framers intended that the Supreme Court would exercise this power in some form; but there is no way of being certain even of that, and it is extremely doubtful that they envisioned the authority in its present form. Nevertheless, although both this right and the right to review state acts were once seriously questioned, they are today firmly entrenched as pillars of the American governmental system, and the American Supreme Court can therefore be described as the most powerful court in the world.

III. PROTECTION OF INDIVIDUAL RIGHTS

The chief protection for the rights of individuals is to be found in Article I, Sections 9 and 10 of the original Constitution and in Amendments One through Eight and Thirteen through Fifteen. Section 9 of Article X is devoted to restrictions on the national government, including the guarantee of the ancient writ of habeas corpus (which prevents detention without trial); the prohibition of bills of attainder or ex post facto laws (which are laws imposing criminal punishment for acts not punishable when performed). Section 10 prohibits bills of attainder or ex post facto laws by the states and also forbids a law impairing the obligation of contracts. For the first half century of the nation's existence this latter provision was the main source of property protection, but judicial construction has today narrowed its scope very considerably. The First Amendment secures the liberty of conscience and expression. While its terms cannot be taken literally to mean that Congress may pass no laws at all touching free expression, it does restrict such legislation. In effect, the amendment requires that Congress refrain from passing such laws unless the Supreme Court regards them as reasonably justified by some public danger. Amendments Four through Eight protect certain procedural rights of the individual—generally speaking, the right to be free from arbitrary treatment by police officers and the right to a fair trial. Amendments Thirteen through Fifteen are the so-called "Civil War Amendments," passed after that conflict largely to ensure the newly freed Negro his civil rights. From the point of view of litigation, the Fourteenth has been by far the most important. For some seventy years after its passage in 1868, the "due process clause" of that Amendment was interpreted chiefly as a protection for property-holders, but today it is construed to restrict the states in somewhat the same way that the first eight Amendments limit the national government.

LETTER OF THE CONVENTION TO CONGRESS

In Convention, September 17, 1787

SIR,

WE HAVE NOW THE HONOR to submit to the consideration of the United States in Congress assembled, that Constitution which has appeared to us the most advisable.

The friends of our country have long seen and desired, that the power of making war, peace, and treaties, of levying money and regulating commerce, and the correspondent executive and judicial authorities should be fully and effectually vested in the general government of the Union: but the impropriety of delegating such extensive trust to one body of men is evident— Hence results the necessity of a different organization.

It is obviously impracticable in the federal government of these States, to secure all rights of independent sovereignty to each, and yet provide for the interest and safety of all— Individuals entering into society, must give up a share of liberty to preserve the rest. The magnitude of the sacrifice must depend as well on situation and circumstances as on the object to be obtained. It is at all times difficult to draw with precision the line between those rights which must be surrendered, and those which may be reserved; and on the present occasion this difficulty was increased by a difference among the several States as to their situation, extent, habits, and particular interests.

In all our deliberations on this subject we kept steadily in our view, that which appears to us the greatest interest of every true American, the consolidation of our Union, in which is involved our prosperity, felicity, safety, perhaps our national existence. This important consideration, seriously and deeply impressed on our minds, led each State in the

Convention to be less rigid on points of inferior magnitude, than might have been otherwise expected; and thus the Constitution, which we now present, is the result of a spirit of amity, and of that of mutual deference and concession which the peculiarity of our political situation rendered indispensable.

That it will meet the full and entire approbation of every State is not perhaps to be expected; but each will doubtless consider, that had her interest alone been consulted, the consequences might have been particularly disagreeable or injurious to others; that it is liable to as few exceptions as could reasonably have been expected, we hope and believe; that it may promote the lasting welfare of that country so dear to us all, and secure her freedom and happiness, is our most ardent wish.

With great respect,

We have the honor to be

SIR,

Your Excellency's most

Obedient and Humble Servants,

GEORGE WASHINGTON, *President*

By Unanimous Order of the Convention
HIS EXCELLENCY
THE PRESIDENT OF CONGRESS

RESOLUTION OF THE CONVENTION

[*September 17, 1787*]

In Convention Monday September 17th, 1787

PRESENT, *The States of New-Hampshire, Massachusetts, Connecticut, Mr. Hamilton from New-York, New Jersey, Pennsylvania, Delaware, Maryland, Virginia, North Carolina, South Carolina, and Georgia.*

Resolved, That the Constitution be laid before the United States in Congress assembled, and that it is the opinion of this convention, that it should afterwards be submitted to a convention of delegates, chosen in each State by the people thereof, under the recommendation of its legislature, for their assent and ratification; and that each convention assenting to, and ratifying the same should give notice thereof to the United States in Congress assembled.

Resolved, That it is the opinion of this convention, that as soon as the conventions of nine States shall have ratified this Constitution, the United States in Congress assembled should fix a day on which electors should be appointed by the States which shall have ratified the same, and a day on which the electors should assemble to vote for the President, and the time and place for commencing proceedings under this Constitution; that after such publication the electors should be appointed, and the senators and representatives elected; that the electors should meet on the day fixed for the election of the President, and should transmit their votes certified, signed, sealed, and directed, as the Constitution requires, to the secretary of the United States in Congress assembled; that the senators and representatives should convene at the time and place assigned; that the senators should appoint a president of the Senate, for the sole purpose of receiving, opening and counting the votes for President; and that after he shall be

45

chosen, the Congress, together with the President, should without delay proceed to execute this Constitution.

By the unanimous order of the convention.

GEORGE WASHINGTON, *President.*

WILLIAM JACKSON, *Secretary.*

THE CONSTITUTION OF THE UNITED STATES

WE THE PEOPLE OF THE UNITED STATES, IN ORDER TO FORM A MORE PERFECT UNION, ESTABLISH JUSTICE, INSURE DOMESTIC TRANQUILITY, PROVIDE FOR THE COMMON DEFENCE, PROMOTE THE GENERAL WELFARE, AND SECURE THE BLESSINGS OF LIBERTY TO OURSELVES AND OUR POSTERITY, DO ORDAIN AND ESTABLISH THIS CONSTITUTION FOR THE UNITED STATES OF AMERICA.

ARTICLE I

SECTION 1. All legislative Powers herein granted shall be vested in a Congress of the United States, which shall consist of a Senate and House of Representatives.

SECTION 2. (1) The House of Representatives shall be composed of Members chosen every second Year by the People of the several States, and the Electors in each State shall have the Qualifications requisite for Electors of the most numerous Branch of the State Legislature.

(2) No person shall be a Representative who shall not have attained to the Age of Twenty-five years, and been seven Years a Citizen of the United States, and who shall not, when elected, be an inhabitant of that State in which he shall be chosen.

(3) Representatives and direct Taxes shall be apportioned among the several States which may be included within this Union, according to their respective Numbers, which shall be determined by adding to the whole Number of free Persons, including those bound to Service for a Term of Years, and excluding Indians not taxed, three fifths of all other Persons. The actual Enumeration shall be made within three Years after the first Meeting of the Congress of the United States, and within every subsequent Term of ten Years, in such Man-

ner as they shall by Law direct. The Number of Representatives shall not exceed one for every thirty Thousand, but each State shall have at Least one Representative; and until such enumeration shall be made, the State of New Hampshire shall be entitled to chuse three, Massachusetts eight, Rhode Island and Providence Plantations one, Connecticut five, New York six, New Jersey four, Pennsylvania eight, Delaware one, Maryland six, Virginia ten, North Carolina five, South Carolina five, and Georgia three.

(4) When vacancies happen in the Representation from any State, the Executive Authority thereof shall issue Writs of Election to fill such Vacancies.

(5) The House of Representatives shall chuse their Speaker and other Officers; and shall have the sole Power of Impeachment.

SECTION 3. (1) The Senate of the United States shall be composed of two Senators from each State, chosen by the Legislature thereof, for six Years; and each Senator shall have one Vote.

(2) Immediately after they shall be assembled in Consequence of the first Election, they shall be divided as equally as may be into three Classes. The Seats of the Senators of the first Class shall be vacated at the Expiration of the second year, of the second Class at the Expiration of the fourth Year, and of the third Class at the Expiration of the sixth Year, so that one third may be chosen every second Year; and if Vacancies happen by Resignation, or otherwise, during the Recess of the Legislature of any State, the Executive thereof may make temporary Appointments until the next meeting of the Legislature, which shall then fill such Vacancies.

(3) No Person shall be a Senator who shall not have attained to the Age of thirty Years, and been nine Years a Citizen of the United States, and who shall not, when elected, be an Inhabitant of that State for which he shall be chosen.

(4) The Vice President of the United States shall be President of the Senate, but shall have no Vote, unless they be equally divided.

(5) The Senate shall chuse their other Officers, and also a President pro tempore, in the Absence of the Vice President, or when he shall exercise the Office of President of the United States.

(6) The Senate shall have the sole Power to try all Impeachments. When sitting for that Purpose, they shall be on Oath or Affirmation. When the President of the United States is tried, the Chief Justice shall preside: And no Person shall be convicted without the Concurrence of two thirds of the Members present.

(7) Judgment in Cases of Impeachment shall not extend further than to removal from Office, and disqualification to hold and enjoy any Office of honor, Trust or Profit under the United States: but the Party convicted shall nevertheless be liable and subject to Indictment, Trial, Judgment and Punishment, according to Law.

SECTION 4. (1) The Times, Places and Manner of holding Elections for Senators and Representatives, shall be prescribed in each State by the Legislature thereof; but the Congress may at any time by Law make or alter such Regulations, except as to the Places of chusing Senators.

(2) The Congress shall assemble at least once in every Year, and such Meeting shall be on the first Monday in December, unless they shall by Law appoint a different Day.

SECTION 5. (1) Each House shall be the Judge of the Elections, Returns and Qualifications of its own Members, and a Majority of each shall constitute a Quorum to do Business; but a smaller Number may adjourn from day to day, and may be authorized to compel the Attendance of absent Members, in such Manner, and under such Penalties as each House may provide.

(2) Each House may determine the Rules of its Proceedings, punish its Members for disorderly Behavior, and, with the Concurrence of two thirds, expel a Member.

(3) Each House shall keep a Journal of its Proceedings, and from time to time publish the same, excepting such Parts as may in their Judgment require Secrecy; and the Yeas and

Nays of the Members of either House on any question shall, at the Desire of one fifth of those present, be entered on the Journal.

(4) Neither House, during the Session of Congress, shall, without the Consent of the other, adjourn for more than three days, nor to any other Place than that in which the two Houses shall be sitting.

SECTION 6. (1) The Senators and Representatives shall receive a Compensation for their Services, to be ascertained by Law, and paid out of the Treasury of the United States. They shall in all Cases, except Treason, Felony and Breach of the Peace, be privileged from Arrest during their Attendance at the Session of their respective Houses, and in going to and returning from the same; and for any Speech or Debate in either House, they shall not be questioned in any other Place.

(2) No Senator or Representative shall, during the Time for which he was elected, be appointed to any civil Office under the Authority of the United States, which shall have been created, or the Emoluments whereof shall have been encreased during such time; and no Person holding any Office under the United States, shall be a Member of either House during his Continuance in Office.

SECTION 7. (1) All Bills for raising Revenue shall originate in the House of Representatives; but the Senate may propose or concur with Amendments as on other Bills.

(2) Every Bill which shall have passed the House of Representatives and the Senate, shall, before it become a Law, be presented to the President of the United States; If he approve he shall sign it, but if not he shall return it, with his Objections to that House in which it shall have originated, who shall enter the Objections at large on their Journal, and proceed to reconsider it. If after such Reconsideration two thirds of that House shall agree to pass the Bill, it shall be sent, together with the Objections, to the other House, by which it shall likewise be reconsidered, and if approved by two thirds of that House, it shall become a Law. But in all such Cases

the Votes of both Houses shall be determined by Yeas and Nays, and the Names of the Persons voting for and against the Bill shall be entered on the Journal of each House respectively. If any Bill shall not be returned by the President within ten Days (Sundays excepted) after it shall have been presented to him, the Same shall be a law, in like Manner as if he had signed it, unless the Congress by their Adjournment prevent its Return, in which Case it shall not be a Law.

(3) Every Order, Resolution, or Vote to which the Concurrence of the Senate and House of Representatives may be necessary (except on a question of Adjournment) shall be presented to the President of the United States; and before the Same shall take Effect, shall be approved by him, or being disapproved by him, shall be repassed by two thirds of the Senate and House of Representatives, according to the Rules and Limitations prescribed in the Case of a Bill.

SECTION 8. (1) The Congress shall have Power To lay and collect Taxes, Duties, Imposts and Excises, to pay the Debts and provide for the common Defence and general Welfare of the United States; but all Duties, Imposts and Excises shall be uniform throughout the United States;

(2) To borrow money on the Credit of the United States;

(3) To regulate Commerce with foreign Nations, and among the several States, and with the Indian Tribes;

(4) To establish an uniform Rule of Naturalization, and uniform Laws on the subject of Bankruptcies throughout the United States;

(5) To coin Money, regulate the Value thereof, and of foreign Coin, and to fix the Standard of Weights and Measures;

(6) To provide for the Punishment of counterfeiting the Securities and current Coin of the United States;

(7) To establish Post Offices and post Roads;

(8) To promote the Progress of Science and useful Arts, by securing for limited Times to Authors and Inventors the exclusive Right to their respective Writings and Discoveries;

(9) To constitute Tribunals inferior to the Supreme Court;

(10) To define and Punish Piracies and Felonies committed

on the high Seas, and Offences against the Law of Nations;

(11) To declare War, grant Letters of Marque and Reprisal, and make Rules concerning Captures on Land and Water;

(12) To raise and support Armies, but no Appropriation of Money to that Use shall be for a longer Term than two Years;

(13) To provide and maintain a Navy;

(14) To make Rules for the Government and Regulation of the land and naval Forces;

(15) To provide for calling forth the Militia to execute the Laws of the Union, suppress Insurrections and repel Invasions;

(16) To provide for organizing, arming, and disciplining, the Militia, and for governing such Part of them as may be employed in the Service of the United States, reserving to the States respectively, the Appointment of the Officers, and the Authority of training the Militia according to the discipline prescribed by Congress;

(17) To exercise exclusive Legislation in all Cases whatsoever, over such District (not exceeding ten Miles square) as may, by Cession of particular States, and the Acceptance of Congress, become the Seat of the Government of the United States, and to exercise like Authority over all Places purchased by the Consent of the Legislature of the State in which the Same shall be, for the Erection of Forts, Magazines, Arsenals, dock-Yards, and other needful Buildings;—And

(18) To make all Laws which shall be necessary and proper for carrying into Execution the foregoing Powers, and all other Powers vested by this Constitution in the Government of the United States, or in any Department or Officer thereof.

SECTION 9. (1) The Migration or Importation of such Persons as any of the States now existing shall think proper to admit, shall not be prohibited by the Congress prior to the Year one thousand eight hundred and eight, but a Tax or Duty may be imposed on such Importation, not exceeding ten dollars for each Person.

(2) The Privilege of the Writ of Habeas Corpus shall not

be suspended unless when in Cases of Rebellion or Invasion the public Safety may require it.

(3) No Bill of Attainder or ex post facto Law shall be passed.

(4) No Capitation, or other direct, tax shall be laid, unless in Proportion to the Census or Enumeration herein before directed to be taken.

(5) No Tax or Duty shall be laid on Articles exported from any State.

(6) No preference shall be given by any Regulation of Commerce or Revenue to the Ports of one State over those of another: nor shall Vessels bound to, or from, one State, be obliged to enter, clear, or pay Duties in another.

(7) No Money shall be drawn from the Treasury, but in Consequence of Appropriations made by Law; and a regular Statement and Account of the Receipts and Expenditures of all public Money shall be published from time to time.

(8) No Title of Nobility shall be granted by the United States: And no Person holding any Office of Profit or Trust under them, shall, without the Consent of the Congress, accept of any present, Emolument, Office, or Title, of any kind whatever, from any King, Prince, or foreign State.

SECTION 10. (1) No State shall enter into any Treaty, Alliance, or Confederation; grant Letters of Marque and Reprisal; coin Money; emit Bills of Credit; make any Thing but gold and silver Coin a Tender in Payment of Debts; pass any Bill of Attainder, ex post facto Law, or Law impairing the Obligation of Contracts, or grant any Title of Nobility.

(2) No State shall, without the Consent of the Congress, lay any Imposts or Duties on Imports or Exports, except what may be absolutely necessary for executing it's inspection Laws: and the net Produce of all Duties and Imposts, laid by any State on Imports or Exports, shall be for the Use of the Treasury of the United States; and all such Laws shall be subject to the Revision and controul of the Congress.

(3) No State shall, without the Consent of Congress, lay any Duty of Tonnage, keep Troops, or Ships of War in time of Peace, enter into any Agreement or Compact with another

State, or with a foreign Power, or engage in War, unless actually invaded, or in such imminent Danger as will not admit of Delay.

ARTICLE II

SECTION 1. (1) The executive Power shall be vested in a President of the United States of America. He shall hold his Office during the Term of four Years, and, together with the Vice President, chosen for the same Term, be elected, as follows:

(2) Each State shall appoint, in such Manner as the Legislature thereof may direct, a Number of Electors, equal to the whole Number of Senators and Representatives to which the State may be entitled in the Congress: but no Senator or Representative, or Person holding an Office of Trust or Profit under the United States, shall be appointed an Elector.

The electors shall meet in their respective States, and vote by ballot for two Persons, of whom one at least shall not be an Inhabitant of the same State with themselves. And they shall make a List of all the Persons voted for, and of the Number of Votes for each; which List they shall sign and certify, and transmit sealed to the Seat of Government of the United States, directed to the President of the Senate. The President of the Senate shall, in the Presence of the Senate and House of Representatives, open all the Certificates, and the Votes shall then be counted. The Person having the greatest Number of Votes shall be the President, if such Number be a Majority of the whole Number of Electors appointed; and if there be more than one who have such Majority and have an equal Number of Votes, then the House of Representatives shall immediately chuse by Ballot one of them for President; and if no person have a Majority, then from the five highest on the List the said House shall in like Manner chuse the President. But in chusing the President, the Votes shall be taken by States, the Representation from each State having one Vote; A quorum for this Purpose shall consist of a Member or Members from two-thirds of the States, and a Majority of all the States shall be necessary to a Choice. In every Case, after the Choice of the President, the person having the greatest Number of Votes of the Electors shall be the Vice President. But if there should remain two or more who have equal votes, the Senate shall chuse from them by Ballot the Vice-President.

(3) The Congress may determine the Time of chusing the Electors, and the Day on which they shall give their Votes; which Day shall be the same throughout the United States.

(4) No Person except a natural born Citizen, or a Citizen of the United States, at the time of the Adoption of this Constitution, shall be eligible to the Office of President; neither shall any Person be eligible to that Office who shall not have attained to the Age of thirty five Years, and been fourteen Years a Resident within the United States.

(5) In Case of the Removal of the President from Office or of his Death, Resignation, or Inability to discharge the Powers and Duties of the said Office, the same shall devolve on the Vice President, and the Congress may by Law provide for the Case of Removal, Death, Resignation, or Inability, both of the President and Vice President, declaring what Officer shall then act as President, and such Officer shall act accordingly, until the Disability be removed, or a President shall be elected.

(6) The President shall, at stated Times, receive for his Services, a Compensation, which shall neither be encreased nor diminished during the Period for which he shall have been elected, and he shall not receive within that Period any other Emolument from the United States, or any of them.

(7) Before he enter on the Execution of his Office, he shall take the following Oath or Affirmation:—"I do solemnly swear (or affirm) that I will faithfully execute the Office of President of the United States, and will to the best of my Ability, preserve, protect and defend the Constitution of the United States."

SECTION 2. (1) The President shall be Commander in Chief

of the Army and Navy of the United States, and of the Militia of the several States, when called into actual Service of the United States; he may require the Opinion, in writing, of the principal Officer in each of the executive Departments, upon any subject relating to the Duties of their respective Offices, and he shall have Power to grant Reprieves and Pardons for Offences against the United States, except in Cases of Impeachment.

(2) He shall have Power, by and with the Advice and Consent of the Senate, to make Treaties, provided two thirds of the Senators present concur; and he shall nominate, and by and with the Advice and Consent of the Senate, shall appoint Ambassadors, other public Ministers and Councils, Judges of the supreme Court, and all other Officers of the United States, whose Appointments are not herein otherwise provided for, and which shall be established by Law: but the Congress may by Law vest the Appointment of such inferior Officers as they think proper, in the President alone, in the Courts of Law, or in the Heads of Departments.

(3) The President shall have power to fill up all Vacancies that may happen during the Recess of the Senate, by granting Commissions which shall expire at the End of their next Session.

SECTION 3.   He shall from time to time give to the Congress Information of the State of the Union, and recommend to their Consideration such Measures as he shall judge necessary and expedient; he may, on extraordinary Occasions, convene both Houses, or either of them, and in Case of Disagreement between them, with Respect to the Time of Adjournment, he may adjourn them to such Time as he shall think proper; he shall receive Ambassadors and other public Ministers; he shall take Care that the Laws be faithfully executed, and shall Commission all the Officers of the United States.

SECTION 4.   The President, Vice President and all civil Officers of the United States, shall be removed from Office on Impeachment for, and Conviction of, Treason, Bribery, or other high Crimes and Misdemeanors.

ARTICLE III

SECTION 1. The judicial Power of the United States, shall be vested in one supreme Court, and in such inferior Courts as the Congress may from time to time ordain and establish. The Judges, both of the supreme and inferior Courts, shall hold their Offices during good Behaviour, and shall, at stated Times, receive for their Services, a Compensation, which shall not be diminished during their Continuance in Office.

SECTION 2. (1) The judicial Power shall extend to all Cases, in Law and Equity, arising under this Constitution, the Laws of the United States, and Treaties made, or which shall be made, under their Authority;—to all Cases affecting Ambassadors, other public Ministers and Consuls;—to all Cases of admiralty and maritime Jurisdiction;—to Controversies to which the United States shall be a party;—to Controversies between two or more States;—between a State and Citizens of another State;—between Citizens of different States,—between Citizens of the same State claiming Lands under Grants of different States, and between a State, or the Citizens thereof, and foreign States, Citizens or subjects.

(2) In all Cases affecting Ambassadors, other public Ministers and Consuls, and those in which a State shall be a Party, the Supreme Court shall have original Jurisdiction. In all the other Cases before mentioned, the supreme Court shall have appellate Jurisdiction, both as to Law and Fact, with such Exceptions, and under such Regulations as the Congress shall make.

(3) The Trial of all Crimes, except in Cases of Impeachment, shall be by Jury; and such Trial shall be held in the State where the said Crimes shall have been committed; but when not committed within any State, the Trial shall be at such Place or Places as the Congress may by Law have directed.

SECTION 3. (1) Treason against the United States, shall consist only in levying War against them, or in adhering to their Enemies, giving them Aid and Comfort. No person shall be convicted of Treason unless on the Testimony of two Witnesses to the same overt Act, or on Confession in open Court.

(2) The Congress shall have Power to declare the Punishment of Treason, but no Attainder of Treason shall work Corruption of Blood, or Forfeiture except during the Life of the Person attainted.

Article IV

Section 1. Full Faith and Credit shall be given in each State to the public Acts, Records, and judicial Proceedings of every other State. And the Congress may by general Laws prescribe the Manner in which such Acts, Records and Proceedings shall be proved, and the Effect thereof.

Section 2. (1) The Citizens of each State shall be entitled to all Privileges and Immunities of Citizens in the several States.

(2) A person charged in any State with Treason, Felony, or other Crime, who shall flee from Justice, and be found in another State, shall on Demand of the executive Authority of the State from which he fled, be delivered up to be removed to the State having Jurisdiction of the Crime.

(3) No person held to Service or Labour in one State, under the Laws thereof, escaping into another, shall, in Consequence of any Law or Regulation therein, be discharged from such Service or Labour, but shall be delivered up on Claim of the Party to whom such service or Labour may be due.

Section 3. (1) New States may be admitted by the Congress into this Union; but no new State shall be formed or erected within the Jurisdiction of any other State; nor any State be formed by the Junction of two or more States, or Parts of States, without the Consent of the Legislatures of the States concerned as well as of the Congress.

(2) The Congress shall have Power to dispose of and make all needful Rules and Regulations respecting the Territory or other Property belonging to the United States; and nothing in this Constitution shall be so construed as to Prejudice

any Claims of the United States, or of any particular State.

Section 4. The United States shall guarantee to every State in this Union a Republican Form of Government, and shall protect each of them against Invasion; and on Application of the Legislature, or of the Executive (when the Legislature cannot be convened) against domestic Violence.

Article V

The Congress, whenever two thirds of both Houses shall deem it necessary, shall propose Amendments to this Constitution, or, on the Application of the Legislatures of two thirds of the several States, shall call a Convention for proposing Amendments, which, in either Case, shall be valid to all Intents and Purposes, as Part of this Constitution, when ratified by the Legislatures of three fourths of the several States, or by Conventions in three fourths thereof, as the one or the other Mode of Ratification may be proposed by the Congress; Provided that no Amendment which may be made prior to the Year One thousand eight hundred and eight shall in any Manner affect the first and fourth Clauses in the Ninth Section of the first Article; and that no State, without its Consent, shall be deprived of its equal Suffrage in the Senate.

Article VI

(1) All Debts contracted and Engagements entered into, before the Adoption of this Constitution, shall be as valid against the United States under this Constitution, as under the Confederation.

(2) This Constitution, and the Laws of the United States which shall be made in pursuance thereof; and all Treaties made, or which shall be made, under the Authority of the United States, shall be the supreme Law of the Land; and the Judges in every State shall be bound thereby, any Thing in the Constitution or Laws of any State to the Contrary notwithstanding.

(3) The Senators and Representatives before mentioned, and the Members of the several State Legislatures, and all executive and judicial Officers, both of the United States and of the several States, shall be bound by Oath or Affirmation, to support this Constitution; but no religious Test shall ever be required as a Qualification to any Office or public Trust under the United States.

ARTICLE VII

The Ratification of the Conventions of nine States, shall be sufficient for the Establishment of this Constitution between the States so ratifying the Same.

DONE in Convention by the Unanimous Consent of the States present the Seventeenth Day of September in the Year of our Lord one thousand seven hundred and Eighty seven and of the Independence of the United States of America the Twelfth. *In Witness* whereof We have hereunto subscribed our Names,

GO. WASHINGTON
Presidt. and Deputy from Virginia.

New Hampshire

JOHN LANGDON   NICHOLAS GILMAN

Massachusetts

NATHANIEL GORHAM   RUFUS KING

Connecticut

WM. SAML. JOHNSON   ROGER SHERMAN

New York

ALEXANDER HAMILTON

New Jersey

WIL: LIVINGSTON   WM. PATTERSON
DAVID BREARLEY   JONA: DAYTON

Pennsylvania

B. Franklin	Thos. Fitzsimons
Thomas Mifflin	Jared Ingersoll
Robt. Morris	James Wilson
Geo. Clymer	Gouv. Morris

Delaware

Geo. Read	Richard Bassett
Gunning Bedford, Jun	Jaco: Broom
John Dickinson	

Maryland

James McHenry	Danl. Carroll
Dan of St. Thos. Jenifer	

Virginia

John Blair	James Madison, Jr

North Carolina

Wm. Blount	Hu. Williamson
Richd Dobbs Spaight	

South Carolina

J. Rutledge	Charles Pinckney
Charles Cotesworth	Pierce Butler
Pinckney.	

Georgia

William Few	Abr. Baldwin
Attest	William Jackson *Secretary*

AMENDMENTS

Articles in Addition to, and Amendment of, the Constitution of the United States of America, Proposed by Congress, and Ratified by the Legislatures of the Several States Pursuant to the Fifth Article of the Original Constitution.

THE FIRST TEN AMENDMENTS: THE BILL OF RIGHTS
[December 15, 1791]

ARTICLE I

Congress shall make no law respecting an establishment of religion, or prohibiting the free exercise thereof; or abridging the freedom of speech, or of the press; or the right of the people peaceably to assemble, and to petition the Government for a redress of grievances.

ARTICLE II

A well regulated Militia, being necessary to the security of a free State, the right of the people to keep and bear Arms, shall not be infringed.

ARTICLE III

No Soldier shall, in time of peace be quartered in any house, without the consent of the Owner, nor in time of war, but in a manner to be prescribed by law.

ARTICLE IV

The right of the people to be secure in their persons, houses, papers, and effects, against unreasonable searches and seizures, shall not be violated, and no Warrants shall issue, but upon probably cause, supported by Oath or affirmation, and particularly describing the place to be searched, and the persons or things to be seized.

ARTICLE . V

No person shall be held to answer for a capital, or otherwise infamous crime, unless on a presentment or indictment of a Grand Jury, except in cases arising in the land or naval forces, or in the Militia, when in actual service in time of War or public danger; nor shall any person be subject for the same offence to be twice put in jeopardy of life or limb; nor shall be compelled in any Criminal Case to be a witness against himself, nor be deprived of life, liberty, or property, without due process of law; nor shall private property be taken for public use, without just compensation.

ARTICLE VI

In all criminal prosecutions, the accused shall enjoy the right to a speedy and public trial, by an impartial jury of the State and district wherein the crime shall have been committed, which district shall have been previously ascertained by law, and to be informed of the nature and cause of the accusation; to be confronted with the witnesses against him; to have compulsory process for obtaining witnesses in his favor, and to have the Assistance of Counsel for his defence.

ARTICLE VII

In Suits at common law, where the value in controversy shall exceed twenty dollars, the right of trial by jury shall be preserved, and no fact tried by a jury, shall be otherwise re-examined in any Court of the United States, than according to the rules of the common law.

Article VIII

Excessive bail shall not be required, nor excessive fines imposed, nor cruel and unusual punishments inflicted.

Article IX

The enumeration in the Constitution, of certain rights, shall not be construed to deny or disparage others retained by the people.

Article X

The powers not delegated to the United States by the Constitution, nor prohibited by it to the States, are reserved to the States respectively, or to the people.

LATER AMENDMENTS

Article XI
[*January 8, 1798*]

The Judicial power of the United States shall not be construed to extend to any suit in law or equity, commenced or prosecuted against one of the United States by Citizens of another State, or by Citizens or Subjects of any Foreign State.

Article XII
[*September 25, 1804*]

The Electors shall meet in their respective states, and vote by ballot for President and Vice-President, one of whom, at least, shall not be an inhabitant of the same state with themselves; they shall name in their ballots the person voted for as President, and in distinct ballots the person voted for as Vice-President, and they shall make distinct lists of all persons voted for as President, and of all persons voted for as Vice-President, and of the number of votes for each, which lists they shall sign and certify, and transmit sealed to the seat of the government of the United States, directed to the President of the Senate;—The President of the Senate shall, in presence of the Senate and House of Representatives, open all the certificates and the votes shall then be counted;—The person having the greatest number of votes for President, shall be the President, if such number be a majority of the whole number of Electors appointed; and if no person have such majority, then from the persons having the highest numbers not exceeding three on the list of those voted for as President, the House of Representatives shall choose immediately, by ballot, the President. But in choosing the President, the votes shall be taken by states, the representation from each state having one vote; a quorum for this purpose shall consist of a member or members from two thirds of the states, and a majority of all the states shall be necessary to a choice. And if the House of Representatives shall not choose a President whenever the right of choice shall devolve upon them, before the fourth day of March next following, then the Vice-President shall act as President, as in the case of the death or other constitutional disability of the President. The person having the greatest number of votes as Vice-President, shall be the Vice-President, if such number be a majority of the whole number of Electors appointed, and if no person have a majority, then from the two highest numbers on the list, the Senate shall choose the Vice-President; a quorum for the purpose shall consist of two thirds of the whole number of Senators, and a majority of the whole number shall be necessary to a choice. But no person constitutionally ineligible to the office of President shall be eligible to that of Vice-President of the United States.

ARTICLE XIII
[December 18, 1865]

Section 1.   Neither slavery nor involuntary servitude, except as a punishment for crime whereof the party shall have been duly convicted, shall exist within the United States, or any place subject to their jurisdiction.

Section 2.   Congress shall have power to enforce this article by appropriate legislation.

ARTICLE XIV
[July 21, 1868]

Section 1.   All persons born or naturalized in the United States, and subject to the jurisdiction thereof, are citizens of the United States and of the State wherein they reside. No State shall make or enforce any law which shall abridge the privileges or immunities of citizens of the United States; nor shall any State deprive any person of life, liberty, or property, without due process of law; nor deny to any person within its jurisdiction the equal protection of the laws.

Section 2.   Representatives shall be apportioned among the several States according to their respective numbers, counting the whole number of persons in each State, excluding Indians not taxed. But when the right to vote at any election for the choice of electors for President and Vice President of the United States, Representatives in Congress, the Executive and Judicial officers of a State, or the members of the Legislature thereof, is denied to any of the male inhabitants of such State, being twenty-one years of age, and citizens of the United States, or in any way abridged, except for participation in rebellion, or other crime, the basis of representation therein shall be reduced in the proportion which the number of such male citizens shall bear to the whole number of male citizens twenty-one years of age in such State.

Section 3.   No person shall be a Senator or Representative

in Congress, or elector of President and Vice President, or hold any office, civil or military, under the United States, or under any State, who, having previously taken an oath, as a member of Congress, or as an officer of the United States, or as a member of any State legislature, or as an executive or judicial officer of any State, to support the Constitution of the United States, shall have engaged in insurrection or rebellion against the same, or given aid or comfort to the enemies thereof. But Congress may by a vote of two thirds of each House, remove such disability.

Section 4. The validity of the public debt of the United States, authorized by law, including debts incurred for payment of pensions and bounties for services in suppressing insurrection or rebellion, shall not be questioned. But neither the United States nor any State shall assume or pay any debt or obligation incurred in aid of insurrection or rebellion against the United States, or any claim for the loss or emancipation of any slave; but all such debts, obligations and claims shall be held illegal and void.

Section 5. The Congress shall have power to enforce, by appropriate legislation, the provisions of this article.

ARTICLE XV
[March 30, 1870]

Section 1. The right of citizens of the United States to vote shall not be denied or abridged by the United States or by any State on account of race, color, or previous condition of servitude.

Section 2. The Congress shall have power to enforce this article by appropriate legislation.

ARTICLE XVI
[February 25, 1913]

The Congress shall have the power to lay and collect taxes on incomes, from whatever source derived, without apportionment among the several States, and without regard to any census or enumeration.

ARTICLE XVII

[May 31, 1913]

Section 1. The Senate of the United States shall be composed of two Senators from each State, elected by the people thereof, for six years; and each Senator shall have one vote. The electors in each State shall have the qualifications requisite for electors of the most numerous branch of the State Legislatures.

Section 2. When vacancies happen in the representation of any State in the Senate, the executive authority of such State shall issue writs of election to fill such vacancies; Provided, That the Legislature of any State may empower the executive thereof to make temporary appointment until the people fill the vacancies by election as the Legislature may direct.

Section 3. This amendment shall not be so construed as to affect the election or term of any Senator chosen before it becomes valid as part of the Constitution.

ARTICLE XVIII

[January 29, 1919]

Section 1. After one year from the ratification of this article, the manufacture, sale, or transportation of intoxicating liquors within, the importation thereof into, or the exportation thereof from the United States and all territory subject to the jurisdiction thereof, for beverage purposes, is hereby prohibited.

Section 2. The Congress and the several States shall have concurrent power to enforce this article by appropriate legislation.

Section 3. This article shall be inoperative unless it shall have been ratified as an amendment to the Constitution by the legislatures of the several States, as provided in the Constitution, within seven years from the date of the submission hereof to the States by the Congress.

ARTICLE XIX
[*August 26, 1920*]

Section 1. The rights of citizens of the United States to vote, shall not be denied or abridged by the United States or by any State on account of sex.

Section 2. Congress shall have power to enforce this article by appropriate legislation.

ARTICLE XX
[*February 6, 1933*]

Section 1. The terms of the President and Vice President shall end at noon on the twentieth day of January, and the terms of Senators and Representatives at noon on the third day of January, of the years in which such terms would have ended if this article had not been ratified; and the terms of their successors shall then begin.

Section 2. The Congress shall assemble at least once in every year, and such meeting shall begin at noon on the third day of January, unless they shall by law appoint a different day.

Section 3. If, at the time fixed for the beginning of the term of the President, the President elect shall have died, the Vice President elect shall become President. If a President shall not have been chosen before the time fixed for the beginning of his term, or if the President elect shall have failed to qualify, then the Vice President elect shall act as President until a President shall have qualified; and the Congress may by law provide for the case wherein neither a President elect nor a Vice President elect shall have qualified, declaring who shall then act as President, or the manner in which one who is to act shall be selected, and such person shall act accordingly until a President or Vice President shall have qualified.

Section 4. The Congress may by law provide for the case of the death of any of the persons from whom the House of Representatives may choose a President whenever the right of choice shall have devolved upon them, and for the case of the death of any of the persons from whom the Senate may choose a Vice President whenever the right of choice shall have devolved upon them.

Section 5. Sections 1 and 2 shall take effect on the fifteenth day of October following the ratification of this article.

Section 6. This article shall be inoperative unless it shall have been ratified as an amendment to the Constitution by the legislatures of three-fourths of the several States within seven years from the date of its submission.

Article XXI
[December 5, 1933]

Section 1. The eighteenth article of amendment to the Constitution of the United States is hereby repealed.

Section 2. The transportation or importation into any State, Territory, or possession of the United States for delivery or use therein of intoxicating liquors, in violation of the laws thereof, is hereby prohibited.

Section 3. This article shall be inoperative unless it shall have been ratified as an amendment to the Constitution by conventions in the several States, as provided in the Constitution, within seven years from the date of the submission hereof to the States by the Congress.

Article XXII
[March 1, 1951]

Section 1. No person shall be elected to the office of the President more than twice, and no person who has held the office of President, or acted as President, for more than two years of a term to which some other person was elected President shall be elected to the office of the President more than once. But this Article shall not apply to any person holding the office of President when this Article was proposed by the Congress, and shall not prevent any person who may be holding the office of President, or acting as President, during the term within which this Article becomes operative from holding the office of President or acting as President during the remainder of such term.

Section 2. This Article shall be inoperative unless it shall have been ratified as an amendment to the Constitution by the Legislatures of three-fourths of the several States within seven years from the date of its submission to the States by the Congress.

The American Heritage Series

The Library of Liberal Arts